fast furniture

ARMAND SUSSMAN

POPULAR WOODWORKING BOOKS

CINCINNATI, OHIO

www.popularwoodworking.com

READ THIS IMPORTANT SAFETY NOTICE

To prevent accidents, keep safety in mind while you work. Use the safety guards installed on power equipment; they are for your protection. When working on power equipment, keep fingers away from saw blades, wear safety goggles to prevent injuries from flying wood chips and sawdust, wear headphones to protect your hearing, and consider installing a dust vacuum to reduce the amount of airborne sawdust in your woodshop. Don't wear loose clothing, such as neckties or shirts with loose sleeves, or jewelry, such as rings, necklaces or bracelets, when working on power equipment. Tie back long hair to prevent it from getting caught in your equipment. People who are sensitive to certain chemicals should check the chemical content of any product before using it. The authors and editors who compiled this book have tried to make the contents as accurate and correct as possible. Plans, illustrations, photographs and text have been carefully checked. All instructions, plans and projects should be carefully read, studied and understood before beginning construction. Due to the variability of local conditions, construction materials, skill levels, etc., neither the author nor Popular Woodworking Books assumes any responsibility for any accidents, injuries, damages or other losses incurred resulting from the material presented in this book.

METRIC CONVERSION CHART

to convert	to	multiply by
Inches	Centimeters	2.54
Centimeters	Inches	0.4
Feet	Centimeters	30.5
Centimeters	Feet	0.03
Yards	Meters	0.9
Meters	Yards	1.1
Sq. Inches	Sq. Centimeters	6.45
Sq. Centimeters	Sq. Inches	0.16
Sq. Feet	Sq. Meters	0.09
Sq. Meters	Sq. Feet	10.8
Sq. Yards	Sq. Meters	0.8
Sq. Meters	Sq. Yards	1.2
Pounds	Kilograms	0.45
Kilograms	Pounds	2.2
Ounces	Grams	28.4
Grams	Ounces	0.04

Fast Furniture. Copyright © 2000 by Armand Sussman. Manufactured in China. All rights reserved. No part of this book may be reproduced in any form or by any electronic or mechanical means including information storage and retrieval systems without permission in writing from the publisher, except by a reviewer, who may quote brief passages in a review. Published by Popular Woodworking Books, an imprint of F&W Publications, Inc., 1507 Dana Avenue, Cincinnati, Ohio, 45207. First edition.

Visit our Web site at www.popularwoodworking.com for information on more resources for woodworkers.

Other fine Popular Woodworking Books are available from your local bookstore or direct from the publisher.

04 03 02 01 00   5 4 3 2 1

Library of Congress Cataloging-in-Publication Data

Sussman, Armand 1918–
    Fast Furniture / by Armand Sussman
        p. cm.
    ISBN 1-55870-543-0
    1. Tables. 2. Furniture making. I. Title.
TT197.5.T3 S87 2000
684.1'3--dc21   00-042783

Projects constructed by Jim Stack
Edited by Michael Berger, Jennifer Churchill
Designed by Brian Roeth
Production coordinated by John Peavler
Page layout by Ben Rucker
Finished projects photographed by Al Parrish
Step-by-step photography by Jim Stack

Location for photography of finished projects provided by Continental Web Press. All projects in this book were constructed in the Popular Woodworking Books woodshop.

About the author

Back in the 1920s and 1930s, when "make do" was a way of life, handsawing and machine sewing were the two hobbies of Armand Sussman. In his pre-teen and teen years, he designed and made his own toys and games, did home repairs and remodeling, and was great at chess and long-distance swimming.

Armand's college education (he was studying to become a math and science teacher) was cut short when he was drafted shortly before the attack on Pearl Harbor. While "stuck" in the infantry, guarding the Panama Canal, he volunteered to join the Army Air Corps in order to get into action. Armand became an officer and earned his wings, enabling him to fly as the navigator on the crew of a "Flying Fortress" B-17 bomber. He navigated over the North Atlantic using only the stars to guide him. He arrived in England to join the 8th Air Force after more than a year of navigation school and crew training.

Two months before D-Day in 1944, while he and his crew were on one of their many bombing missions over Germany, his plane was destroyed by flak and fighter planes. All 10 crewmen, some wounded, bailed out and all were captured as P.O.W.s for 13 months.

After WWII, from 1946–1952, Armand managed an 80-employee sewing plant. Then he put his woodworking hobby to work, selling nationally by mail-order the home furnishings he designed and made.

In the mid-1950s, Armand was a designer for a corrugated container manufacturer. In 1957, he opened a clothing store from which he retired in 1992 at age 74. However, he continued designing, making and writing about wooden home furnishings. He is still expanding on his concept of woodworking — using only sticks and glue to create a variety of unique home furnishings.

Dedication

To my neighbors, who never complain about my favorite sound: the noise that my table saw makes at some "crazy-hour" times. I am also grateful to the kids playing in the back alley who offset my table-saw noise with other favorite sounds of mine: their laughter, yelling, squealing, and some screaming, during the no-school summer months.

My most heartfelt dedication goes to the guys and gals for whom I have written this book.

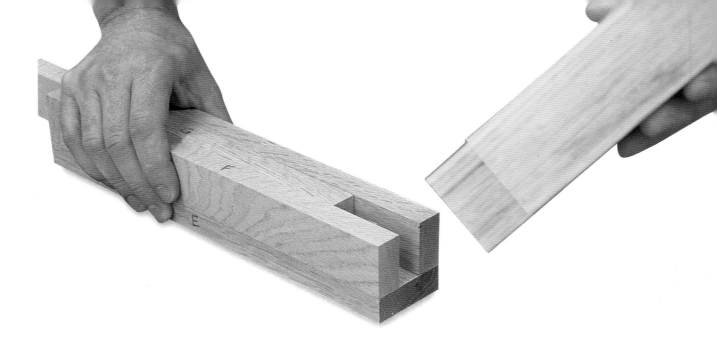

table of contents

introduction

Fast furniture is made from materials you're likely to have in your woodworking shop. As a youngster, long before the days of conservation awareness, I was programmed by the deprivation of the 1930s not to throw away a piece of wood even a few inches long. I became a saver of "maybes" (maybe I'll need it). Years later I realized the pile of "maybes" in my woodworking shop had grown too large. One day, as I sat staring at the pile of scrap lumber, I thought, why not make furniture from sticks? It would be simple, inexpensive, sturdy and even attractive. My pulse quickened with the possibilities. It would be a total departure from most woodworking methods and easy to be creative. The only materials needed would be glue and wood sticks.

In these projects, we have just flat sticks — all the same thickness and width but with different lengths — cut with squared ends; no angles, curves or grooves. So how can you make a useful furnishing or accessory from just plain sticks? Every project has detailed instructions on how to build a piece of furniture made just from sticks and glue that will intrigue your family and friends. You can also tailor the projects to the sizes you might need. Upscale a table for four to a table for eight, or a snapshot-size picture frame to a 6' x 10' mural frame.

Most of the projects in this book are original designs and some are versions of common pieces of furniture and accessories. You don't have to get involved in creating complex furniture and cabinetmaking joints such as dovetails, dowels, miters and mortise and tenon: When three sticks of $\frac{3}{4}$" x $2\frac{1}{4}$" are glued together face-to-face while keeping all edges flush, a laminated square chunk of wood $2\frac{1}{4}$" x $2\frac{1}{4}$" is created. It can be used for a leg or an apron in a piece of stick furniture. By varying the lengths of the individual sticks that make up each piece, many common woodworking joints can be created. These project assembly methods are unique. As you progress through the projects, I hope your project construction will be enjoyable and rewarding.

tips for getting started

Whoever first said "there's a trick to everything" must have been a woodworker. How many times have unexpected pitfalls or problems reared their ugly heads just when you thought you were on the home stretch with your project? Well, fear not, for before we dive into the projects themselves, I want to take a moment to show you some time-saving — and headache-saving — tips, tricks and techniques that will make each project that much more simple and trouble-free to construct. Through years of building these projects, these are the best ways I've found to preserve my sanity and still be able to achieve spectacular results time after time.

Table Saw Sled Construction

The table saw is perfect for making accurate and repetitive crosscuts. This crosscut sled is the best tool for making those cuts safely and easily. It's large enough to make a 24" crosscut. The adjustable stop has a flipper, so only one setting is necessary to cut both ends of a board to length.

Cut the sled table to size and rout the two handle slots. Center the sled on the saw table, locate the left milled slot in the saw top and mark its location on the sled. At the mark, draw a line square to the long edge of the sled table. Mount one runner along the line with flathead screws. Put the sled on the table saw and fine-tune the fit of the runner using a scraper or chisel. When it slides smoothly in the slot, mark the location of the other slot. Mount the second runner and check the fit on the table saw. When the sled slides smoothly, apply wax to the underside.

Cut the front fence and rear stiffener pieces and shape per the drawing. Cut the slot in the front fence and mill a ¼" × ¼" rabbet on the bottom inside edge. Center the rear stiffener on the sled and attach it with 2" screws. Center the front fence and attach it at each end using screws in slotted holes. Raise the saw blade, set the sled in place and carefully cut the kerf in the sled. Set a carpenter's square against the front fence and adjust the fence until it is square to the saw kerf. Square the fence vertically to the sled table and attach with 2" screws. Cut and shape the safety block and attach it to the sled.

With the stop-block cut to size, set it against the inside of the front fence and mark the hole for the carriage bolt so it lines up with the slot. Set the bolt in the block, check the fit of the block to the fence and attach the knob. Attach the flipper so it can be pivoted up and freely dropped back into place.

Accuracy in Milling

Strive for accuracy in milling the materials you'll need, whether you make them yourself or have them done at a planing mill. Uniform thickness of the sticks you prepare is of the utmost importance, as is cutting the lengths and widths accurately. As easy as making step-miter frames can be, errors show up as gaps, most often because of varying thicknesses in the pieces.

Assembly Jigs

Assembly jigs greatly aid in assembly by helping you get everything aligned. By using these jigs in conjunction with the cutting lists and the technical drawings, you can ensure a high degree of accuracy. The leg jig is handy for assembly of smaller parts, while the large jig is useful for assembling larger sections, such as tops. Use the following dimensions to construct your own jigs.

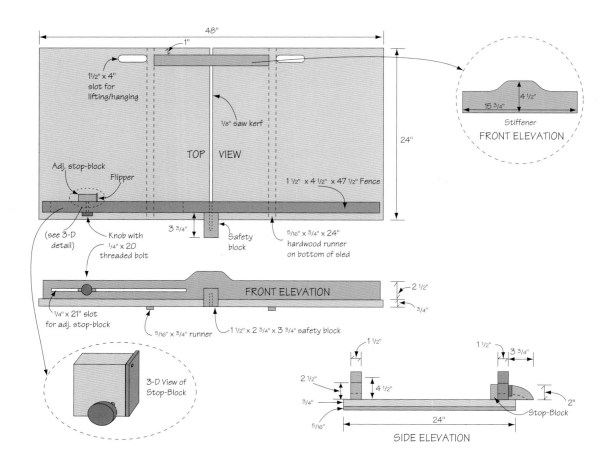

[CUTTING LIST] *Table Saw Jig*

REF.	QTY.	PART	MATERIAL	THICK	WIDTH	LENGTH	COMMENTS
	1	Table	Plywood	¾	24	48	
	1	Front Fence	Plywood	1½	4½	47½	Glue up two ¾" pieces for thickness
	1	Rear Stiffener	Plywood	1½	4½	15¾	Glue up two ¾" pieces for thickness
	2	Runners	Hardwood	⁵⁄₁₆	¾	24	
	1	Safety Block	Plywood	1½	2¾	3¾	Glue up two ¾" pieces for thickness

HARDWARE

	17	no. 6 2" Drywall Screws
	1	¼" × 2½" × 20 Carriage Bolt
	1	¼" Fender Washer
	1	¼" × 20 Threaded Knob

Leg Jig

Back   ¾" × 3" × 31¼" melamine
Bottom   ¾" × 3" × 31¼" melamine
End   ¾" × 3" × 3¾" melamine

Screw the back to the bottom, checking for 90° where the two pieces meet. Screw the side onto the end of the side-and-bottom assembly, again checking for 90° where the pieces meet. It is very important that these jigs are accurate. The gluing-up of subassemblies with good and accurate joints will pay off at the final project assembly.

Large Jig

Back   ¾" × 4" × 48¾" melamine
Side   ¾" × 4" × 36" melamine
Bottom   ¾" × 35¼" × 48" melamine

Screw the side to the bottom, checking for 90° where the two pieces meet. Screw the back onto the side-and-bottom assembly, checking for 90° where the bottom and back meet and where the side meets the back. This jig will be used for gluing-up the subassemblies and will make it much easier to handle everything.

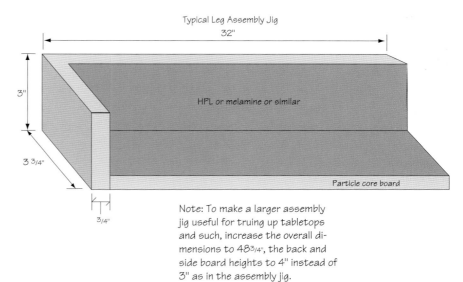

Typical Leg Assembly Jig
32"
3"
3 ¾"
¾"
HPL or melamine or similar
Particle core board

Note: To make a larger assembly jig useful for truing up tabletops and such, increase the overall dimensions to 48¾", the back and side board heights to 4" instead of 3" as in the assembly jig.

Precision Assembly

Before final glue-up, dry fit all parts so any gaps or other inaccuracies can be found. The edges and ends of all the parts must be square, sharp, free of dust and splinters, and the lengths cut accurately. Organize all parts into groups that will be glued together (as shown in the photo to the right), and note which surfaces will receive the glue once the parts are assembled.

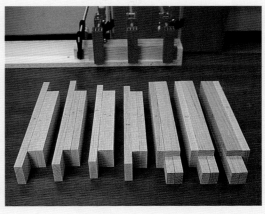

Clamps

We know that no shop can have too many clamps, but these projects can be assembled using a minimum of five to six clamps. The clamps should have pads on the clamping surfaces to protect the wood from being marred. Scrapwood blocks can be used as pads if necessary. The blocks can be taped to the clamp faces or just placed between the clamp faces and the work. Use only enough clamping pressure to hold parts in place while the glue dries. Too much pressure can force too much glue out of the joint and it could fail. Worse yet, clamps can be bent and ruined.

Glue

Any of the yellow or brown wood glues (aliphatic resin glue) will work on these projects. If you want longer working time (time until the glue starts setting), use polyurethane glues that are now available at local home-improvement stores. They require a longer clamping time (2 to 4 hours). This type of glue is recommended for the end-grain step-miter joints used to assemble many of the projects in this book. It has superior holding power over all other wood glues.

Glass and Other Tops

The tables in this book have open tops. They function very well when used with a glass top. Glass gives the illusion of space while providing utility. The unique designs of these tables

Cleaning Up Glue
Once the glue becomes rubbery, use a chisel to clean out the excess glue that squeezed out when you clamped the parts together.

can be seen very clearly and they function very well as tables.

Glass comes in clear, bronze, gray and other translucent colors. It also comes in a variety of thicknesses, including $\frac{3}{16}$", $\frac{1}{4}$", $\frac{3}{8}$" and $\frac{1}{2}$". It can be cut into any shape, such as square, oval, circle, hexagon, octagon, etc. The edges of glass can be polished after the top has been cut. This polishing makes the edges smooth and safe to the touch and also adds a very nice look. These edges can be slightly rounded in shape, flat-polished, beveled or bullnosed (a half-rounded shape). Small holes ($\frac{1}{16}$") up to large circle cutouts in the glass also can be special-ordered. Use only tempered or safety glass for table tops.

Other materials may be used for tops, including painted MDF (medium-density fiberboard) and veneered

Table Height Specifications

Dining tables are 29" or 30" high and 24" for each person is needed for seating. The height of desks is 29". Foyer, cocktail and console tables are 20" to 24" high. Sofa, end, bedside, TV and lamp tables are 25" to 27" high. Coffee tables are 14" to 18" high. Footrests are 12" to 14" high.

plywood. Plywood can have hardwood edges applied and routed into a profile or left square. MDF can be cut into any shape, profiled on the edges and sanded smooth, creating an excellent surface for painting.

Holes can easily be drilled, and larger holes can be routed, to accept glass or mirrors.

Sanding

When the glue has set and the clamps have been removed from the project, the next order of business is getting the project ready to be finished. Use a block plane to level any parts of the assembly that are too uneven to be sanded easily ($\frac{1}{32}$" or greater is a good rule of thumb). A sharp plane will easily trim end grain as well as long grain, so use it to do the bulk of the leveling.

A random-orbit sander is the best tool to use for sanding the projects in this book. Start sanding with 100-grit sandpaper to do the basic leveling and to even all surfaces. Keep the sander flat, use light pressure and keep the tool moving so there won't be any dips in the sanded surface. (I recommend practicing with the sander on scrap pieces to learn how the tool feels and how it moves. Using hand power tools requires practice, just like learning to use a hand plane or scraper). To sand the inside corners, use a hard sanding block (made of a block of wood 1" × 3" × 5½" that has been milled flat; a piece of MDF or like material will work very well also). The sanding block will get the sandpaper right into the corners and even the surface out to where the power sander left off. The purpose of

Calculating Board Feet

To determine the board feet in any given project, follow these simple steps:

1. Add up the lengths, in inches, for each individual width of lumber needed for your project.

2. Multiply each individual width, in inches, by the total length, in inches, needed for that width (the number you added up in step 1). This gives you the square inches needed for each individual width.

3. Add together the square inches of all the different widths in your project.

4. Divide that number by 144 (the total number of inches in a square foot). The result is the total square feet (also known as board feet) needed for your project (a board foot is 12" x 12" x 1").

this first sanding is to level the surface and give it an even grade of smoothness. Change to 120-grit sandpaper and sand the surface to eliminate the scratches of the 100-grit paper. Sand into the corners as before and then move on to the final 150-grit sandpaper. This final sanding eliminates the scratches left from previous sandings. Remember that the surface is already level, so light sanding is all that is needed. To more easily show any imperfections, wipe the surface with lacquer thinner and see if any scratches stand out. If so, repeat final sanding again and the project should be ready for the finishing stage.

Finishing

Fear starts to creep into the hearts of many woodworkers when the word *finishing* comes up. Fear not! I've shown you the best way to get the project surface ready for finishing by sanding progressively through sandpaper grits. If the wood surface is smooth and even in appearance and all the swirly scratches have been removed, you are ready to apply the finish.

There are two basic methods of applying finish; with a brush or cloth, and spraying. If you have the setup to spray (spray booth or room, exhaust fan, compressor, spray gun), then you simply shoot a sanding sealer and sand it with 220-grit sandpaper to smooth it. Then shoot a topcoat of lacquer or polyurethane. Nitrocellulose lacquer builds slowly and will blend with itself with each coat that is added, creating one thick finish that can be sanded smooth and rubbed out with #0000 steel wool. For a more durable finish, I recommend a urethane finish. When using urethane, do not use a sanding sealer. Just apply the urethane and it will seal itself. Let it dry 24 hours and sand with 220-grit sandpaper and apply a topcoat. Let that dry 24 to 48 hours. Sand if it is not smooth with 220-grit sandpaper and then rub out with #0000 steel wool. (Note: urethane dries to a very hard finish. Rubbing it out will re-

quire more work than with lacquer. It would be better to make sure that your topcoat is put on as dust-free as possible so it will dry smoothly.)

If you have a small workshop, like most of us, you'll want to use a rub-on finish. The oil and urethane combination finish is recommended. It can be applied with a rag, brush or foam applicator. Pour some of the finish into a separate container and work from that (this will keep the finish in the original container from being contaminated). Saturate the surface with this oil combination and then wipe off the excess that does not soak into the wood. Let it dry 24 hours and then lightly sand it with 220-grit sandpaper and repeat the application procedure. This finish will start building after two to three coats. Apply as many coats as you need to get the sheen you like. I recommend three coats sanded with 220-grit sandpaper and rubbed out with #0000 steel wool. This will provide the water-resistant finish suitable for these projects.

If you want to stain your projects, sand a few scrap pieces of wood just as you have sanded your projects. Choose the stain you want and test it on one of the scraps. I recommend oil-based stains for good penetration into the wood. These stains do not dry as quickly as the water-based stains, so your working time is a little longer. Apply the stain with a rag, brush or foam applicator. Wipe off all the excess stain that doesn't soak into the wood. The color of the stain can be regulated by using a rag that is damp with stain. Use it to wipe off the stain gently, as if you are painting the stain onto the wood. This requires a little practice, but you have scrap pieces to work with! Let the stain dry for 24 hours before applying any finish. When it is dry, proceed as explained above with your finishing.

basic parsons
TABLE

This table measures 18" wide by 18" long by 18" high.

It is based on the original Parsons table designed by

students at the Parsons School of Design in New York

City. The method of construction makes this table an

original. It can function as an end table or a night stand

or even a small coffee table. This project is made of red

oak with a clear finish and is moderately easy to build.

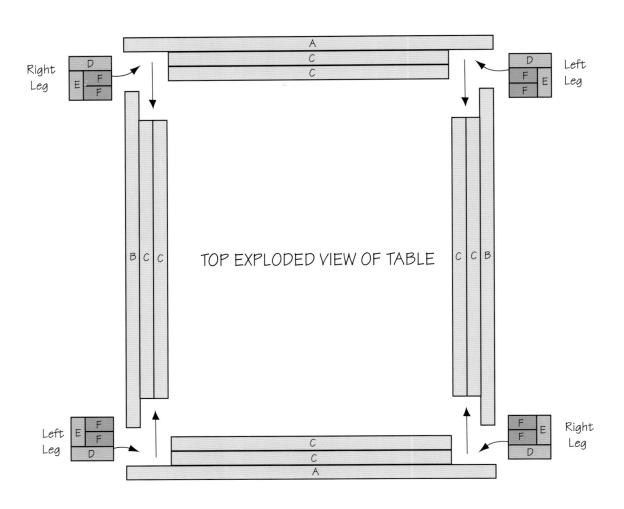

Right Leg

Left Leg

TOP EXPLODED VIEW OF TABLE

Left Leg

Right Leg

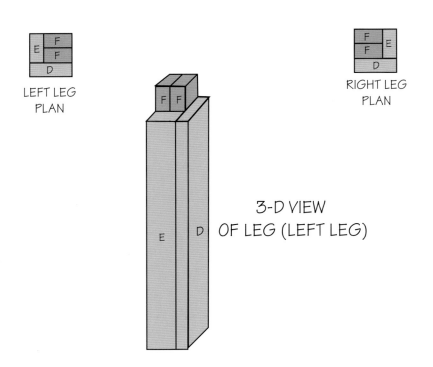

LEFT LEG PLAN

RIGHT LEG PLAN

3-D VIEW OF LEG (LEFT LEG)

[CUTTING LIST] *18" Basic Parsons Table*

REF.	QTY.	PART	MATERIAL	THICK	WIDTH	LENGTH	COMMENTS
A	2	Top	Oak	$3/4$	$2^{1}/_{4}$	18	
B	2	Top	Oak	$3/4$	$2^{1}/_{4}$	$16^{1}/_{2}$	
C	8	Top	Oak	$3/4$	$2^{1}/_{4}$	$13^{1}/_{2}$	
D	4	Legs	Oak	$3/4$	$2^{1}/_{4}$	$15^{3}/_{4}$	
E	4	Legs	Oak	$3/4$	$1^{1}/_{2}$	$15^{3}/_{4}$	
F	8	Legs	Oak	$3/4$	$1^{1}/_{2}$	18	

[CUTTING LIST] *15" Basic Parsons Table*

REF.	QTY.	PART	MATERIAL	THICK	WIDTH	LENGTH	COMMENTS
A	2	Top	Oak	$3/4$	$2^{1}/_{4}$	15	
B	2	Top	Oak	$3/4$	$2^{1}/_{4}$	$13^{1}/_{2}$	
C	8	Top	Oak	$3/4$	$2^{1}/_{4}$	$10^{1}/_{2}$	
D	4	Legs	Oak	$3/4$	$2^{1}/_{4}$	$12^{3}/_{4}$	
E	4	Legs	Oak	$3/4$	$1^{1}/_{2}$	$12^{3}/_{4}$	
F	8	Legs	Oak	$3/4$	$1^{1}/_{2}$	15	

tip

Any of the projects in this book can be built to any size you like. As an example, two sets of dimensions are shown here — one for the standard 18" table, and one for a slightly smaller 15" version.

1

2

3

As shown in these four photos, use
the leg jig to glue up the apron ACC.
Space the pieces using a 2¼" spacer. (BCC aprons are glued up similarly
but use a 1½" spacer.) Two of each
of these assemblies are needed.

4

PROJECT *one*

Glue up legs DEFF (Make two [2] left and two [2] right if end-grain alignment is wanted), as shown in photos 5 through 7. Four (4) legs are needed.

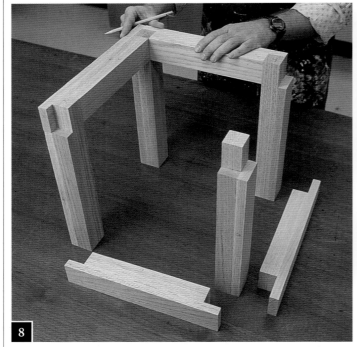

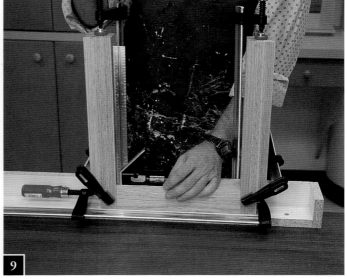

As shown in photo 8, dry fit the table to see how and if it will all go together. Be sure to label all the parts. Then make the leg/apron assembly by using apron BCC and a left leg and a right leg, as in photo 9. Two (2) of these assemblies are needed.

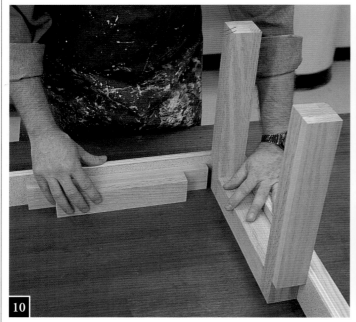

Photos 10 through 22 show the final assembly of the table. Glue the two (2) ACC aprons to the two (2) leg/apron assemblies.

16

17

18

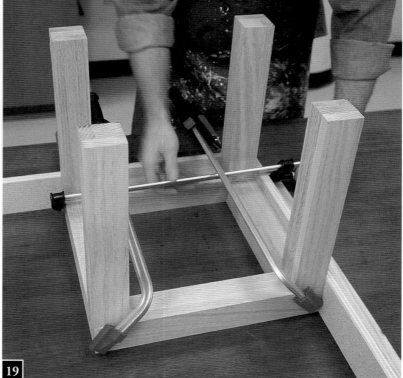

19

Photos 21 and 22 demonstrate that
when the diagonal measurements are
equal, you know the table is square.

evolution
TABLE

This table measures 18" wide by 18" long by 18" high. The first time I built this table a buddy of mine said, "Man, this is evolution. First the monkey on all fours and now man on two feet." Then he asked if the table was stable and strong. I didn't know. The glued table had been setting for several days. I leaned over and put my hands on the outside corner (the one without a leg). I let all of my 160 pounds lean on this corner and I lifted myself completely off the floor. There were no creaking sounds from the table. There wasn't a sound from either of us, either. I was more surprised than my buddy that the table didn't crack or break! This project is made of red oak and stained a light walnut color. It is moderately easy to build.

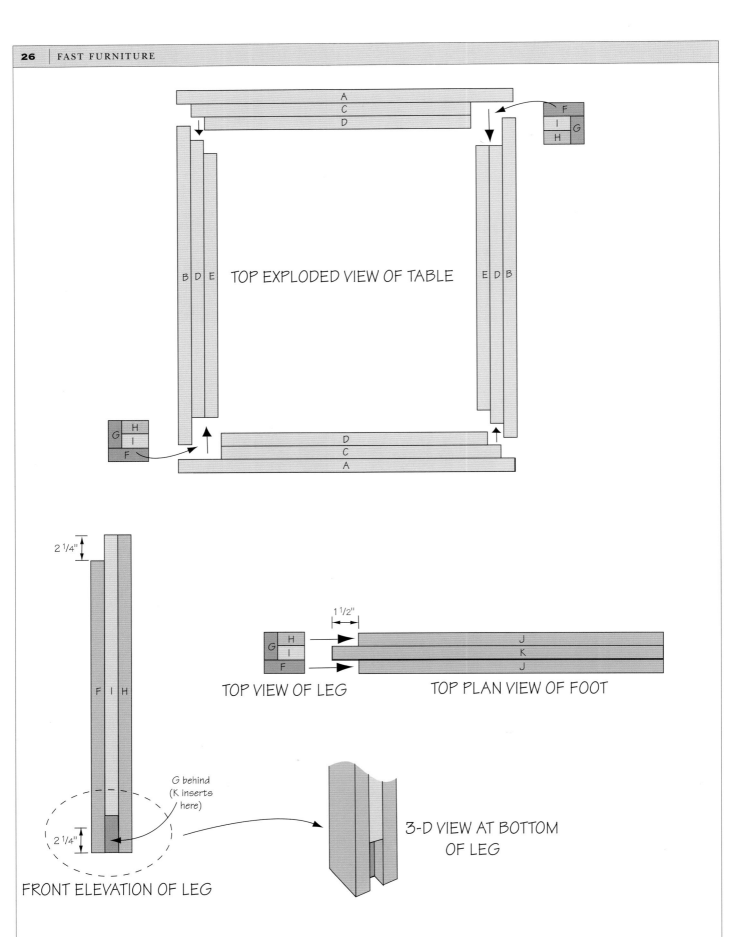

TOP EXPLODED VIEW OF TABLE

2 1/4"

1 1/2"

TOP VIEW OF LEG

TOP PLAN VIEW OF FOOT

G behind
(K inserts
here)

3-D VIEW AT BOTTOM
OF LEG

2 1/4"

FRONT ELEVATION OF LEG

[CUTTING LIST] *Evolution Table*

REF.	QTY.	PART	MATERIAL	THICK	WIDTH	LENGTH	COMMENTS
A	2	Top	Oak	3/4	2 1/4	15	
B	2	Top	Oak	3/4	2 1/4	13 1/2	
C	2	Top	Oak	3/4	2 1/4	12	
D	4	Top	Oak	3/4	2 1/4	11 1/4	
E	2	Top	Oak	3/4	2 1/4	10 1/2	
F	2	Legs	Oak	3/4	2 1/4	12 3/4	
G	2	Legs	Oak	3/4	1 1/2	12 3/4	
H	2	Legs	Oak	3/4	1 1/2	15	
I	2	Legs	Oak	3/4	1 1/2	12 3/4	
J	4	Feet	Oak	3/4	2 1/4	12 3/4	
K	2	Feet	Oak	3/4	2 1/4	14 1/4	

Glue up rails ACD and BDE with a step-miter joint. Using two jigs set square to each other makes this operation easy. (Note the 1½" spacer and the 2¼" spacer at the ends of the aprons. These create the notches for the legs.) Two (2) of these assemblies are needed.

Using this same jig setup, leg FGHI and foot JKJ are glued together to form a leg/foot assembly. Two (2) of these assemblies are needed.

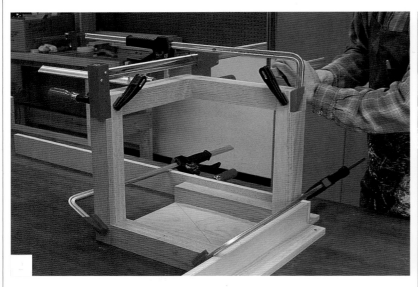

Glue-up of the two (2) leg assemblies and one (1) apron assembly. (Note the use of a square piece of plywood and two gluing jigs squared to each other. The bottom clamps hold the table in place against the jigs.)

Detail of clamping the apron and legs.

Put glue on all surfaces that come into contact with each other when the joint is put together.

Final glue-up of the two (2) leg/foot assemblies and the two (2) ACD-BDE apron assemblies.

ONE-LEG *table*

This table is 18" long by 18" wide by 18" high and is
another original variation on the Basic Parsons Table.
It gives the illusion of having one leg when viewed at
various angles. It is strong but has a light look. This
project is made of red oak with a clear finish and is
moderately difficult to build.

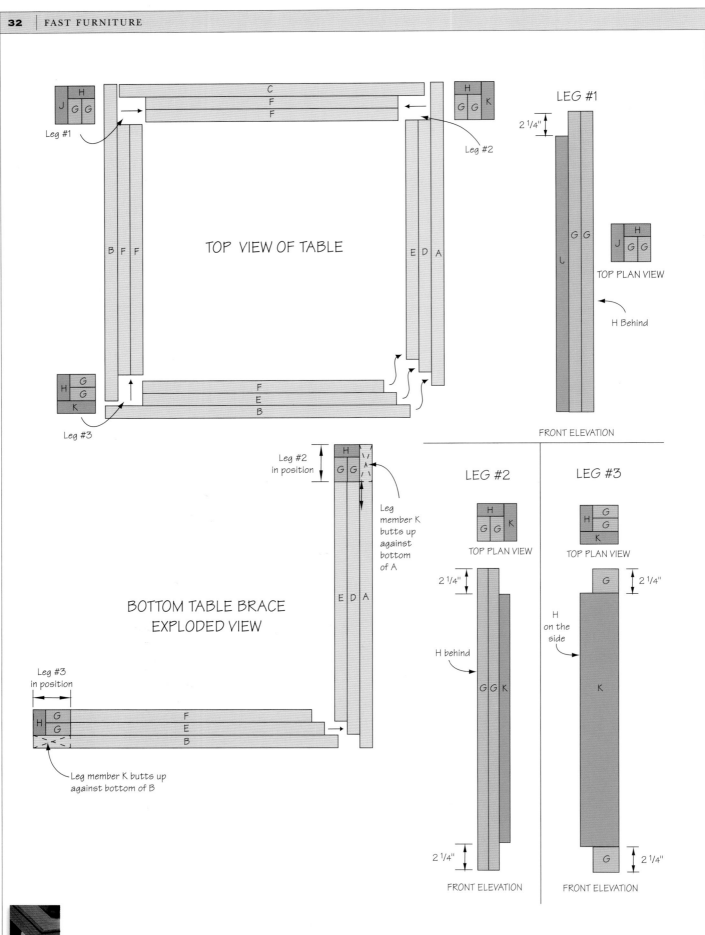

LEG #1

2 1/4"

TOP VIEW OF TABLE

Leg #1

Leg #2

Leg #3

TOP PLAN VIEW

H Behind

FRONT ELEVATION

Leg #2
in position

Leg member K
butts up
against
bottom
of A

LEG #2

LEG #3

TOP PLAN VIEW

TOP PLAN VIEW

BOTTOM TABLE BRACE
EXPLODED VIEW

2 1/4"

2 1/4"

H behind

H
on the
side

Leg #3
in position

Leg member K butts up
against bottom of B

2 1/4"

2 1/4"

FRONT ELEVATION

FRONT ELEVATION

[CUTTING LIST] *One-Leg Table*

REF.	QTY.	PART	MATERIAL	THICK	WIDTH	LENGTH	COMMENTS
A	2	Table	Oak	$3/4$	$2^{1}/4$	18	
B	3	Table	Oak	$3/4$	$2^{1}/4$	$17^{1}/4$	
C	1	Table	Oak	$3/4$	$2^{1}/4$	$16^{1}/2$	
D	2	Table	Oak	$3/4$	$2^{1}/4$	15	
E	4	Table	Oak	$3/4$	$2^{1}/4$	$14^{1}/4$	
F	6	Table	Oak	$3/4$	$2^{1}/4$	$13^{1}/2$	
G	6	Legs 1, 2, 3	Oak	$3/4$	$1^{1}/2$	18	
H	3	Legs 1, 2, 3	Oak	$3/4$	$1^{1}/2$	$15^{3}/4$	
J	1	Leg 1	Oak	$3/4$	$2^{1}/4$	$15^{3}/4$	
K	2	Legs 2, 3	Oak	$3/4$	$2^{1}/4$	$13^{1}/2$	

Glue-up of the top rail BFF using the 2¼" spacer.

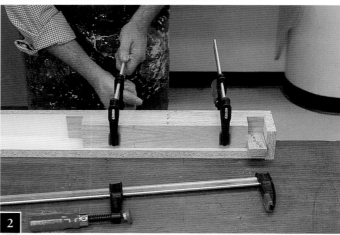

Glue-up of the top rail CFF using the 1½" spacer.

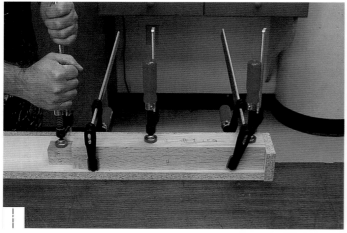

Glue-up of leg 1 (GGHJ). (See the illustration for leg 1.)

Glue-up of leg 2 (GGHK). (See the illustration for leg 2.)

Glue-up of leg 3 (GGHK). (See the illustration for leg 3. It uses the same lettered parts as leg 2 but is configured differently.)

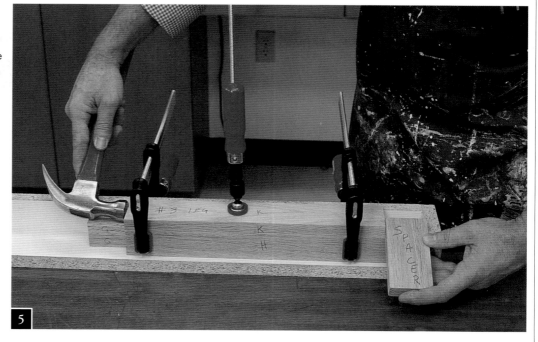

Glue together aprons BEF and EDA using a step-miter joint. (The glue-up of leg 1 to apron CFF is done similarly to the glue-up of the BEF and EDA aprons using jigs squared to each other.)

Glue legs 2 and 3 to two (2) BEF and EDA foot and apron assemblies.

Glue leg 1 assembly and apron BFF to the rest of the table assembly.

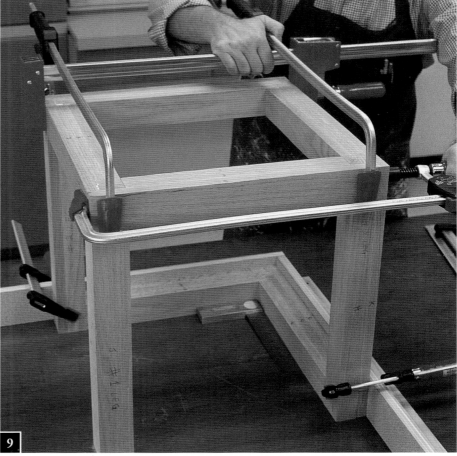

Clamp the final assembly together.

tri-cube
COFFEE TABLE

This table is 15" wide by 40½" long by 15" high and is
an original design. It expands even further upon the
Basic Parsons Table by combining two tables into one,
but it actually looks like three! It is difficult to build because it takes a great deal of concentration to keep all
the parts in order, but the effort is worth the results. It
is made of red oak with a clear finish.

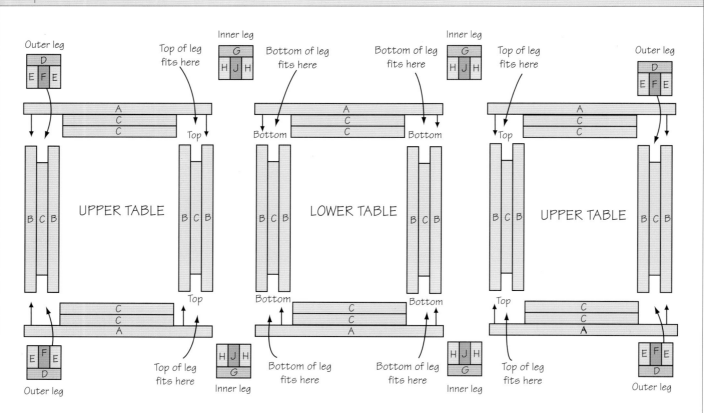

Outer leg

Top of leg fits here

Inner leg

Bottom of leg fits here

Bottom of leg fits here

Inner leg

Top of leg fits here

Outer leg

Top

Bottom

Bottom

Top

UPPER TABLE

LOWER TABLE

UPPER TABLE

Top

Bottom

Bottom

Top

Outer leg

Top of leg fits here

Inner leg

Bottom of leg fits here

Bottom of leg fits here

Inner leg

Top of leg fits here

Outer leg

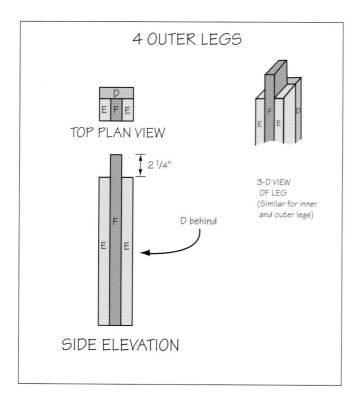

4 OUTER LEGS

TOP PLAN VIEW

2 1/4"

3-D VIEW OF LEG
(Similar for inner and outer legs)

D behind

SIDE ELEVATION

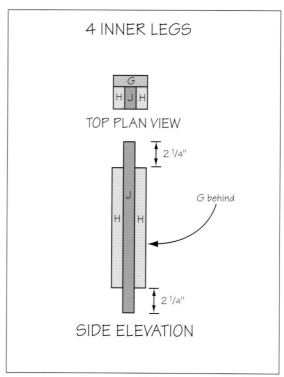

4 INNER LEGS

TOP PLAN VIEW

2 1/4"

G behind

2 1/4"

SIDE ELEVATION

PROJECT *four*

[CUTTING LIST] *Tri-Cube Coffee Table*

REF.	QTY.	PART	MATERIAL	THICK	WIDTH	LENGTH	COMMENTS
A	6	Tables	Red Oak	$3/4$	$2^{1}/4$	15	
B	12	Tables	Red Oak	$3/4$	$2^{1}/4$	$13^{1}/2$	
C	18	Tables	Red Oak	$3/4$	$2^{1}/4$	$10^{1}/2$	
D	4	Outer Legs	Red Oak	$3/4$	$2^{1}/4$	$12^{3}/4$	
E	8	Outer Legs	Red Oak	$3/4$	$1^{1}/2$	$12^{3}/4$	
F	4	Outer Legs	Red Oak	$3/4$	$1^{1}/2$	15	
G	4	Inner Legs	Red Oak	$3/4$	$2^{1}/4$	$10^{1}/2$	
H	8	Inner Legs	Red Oak	$3/4$	$1^{1}/2$	$10^{1}/2$	
J	4	Inner Legs	Red Oak	$3/4$	$1^{1}/2$	15	

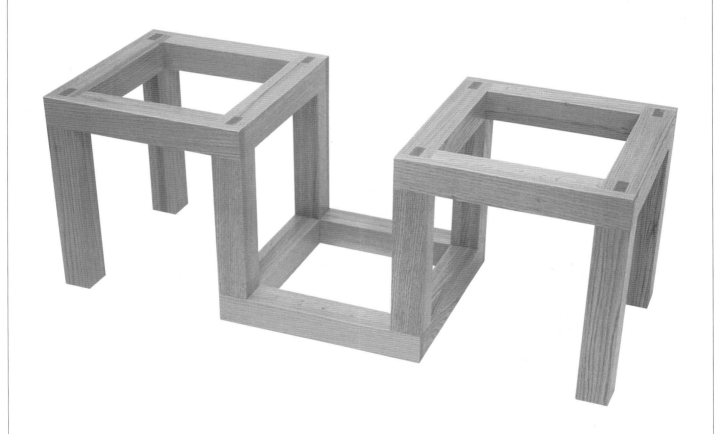

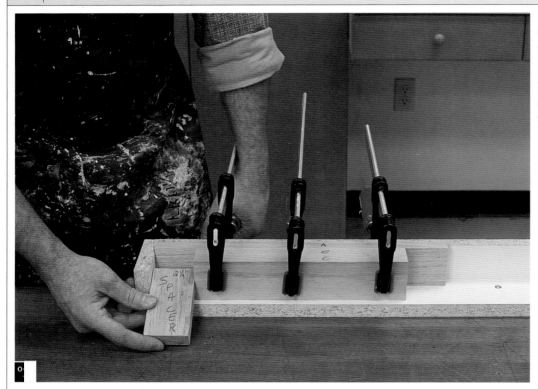

Glue-up of ACC feet and aprons using the 2¼" spacer. Six (6) of these assemblies are needed. The glue-up of the outer legs DEEF is similar to the ACC assemblies. Four (4) each of these legs are needed.

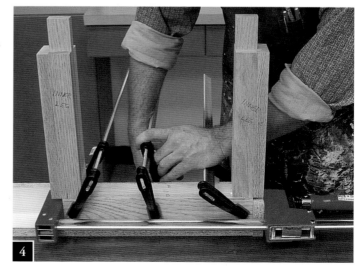

As shown in photos 2 through 4, glue up two (2) inner legs GHHJ and foot assembly BCB. (Note that the foot assembly is loose until glue-up. It is easier to capture the tenon on the legs at this point in the assembly.) Four (4) assemblies (two [2] inner and two [2] outer) are needed.

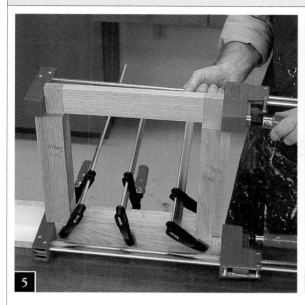

Photos 5 through 7 show the glue-up of inner apron BCB to inner leg assembly. Glue the center piece C into place first.

Glue on the two outside pieces B last. Make two (2) assemblies like this as shown in photos 6 and 7.

Glue up two (2) outer leg DEEF assemblies to loose apron assembly BCB. Make two (2) of these outer leg/apron assemblies.

Use two (2) ACC apron assemblies to glue up an inner leg/apron assembly to an outer leg/apron assembly. Two (2) of these inner/outer leg/apron assemblies are needed.

Final clamping for the inner/outer leg/apron assemblies.

Glue the two inner/outer leg/apron assemblies together using two (2) ACC foot assemblies.

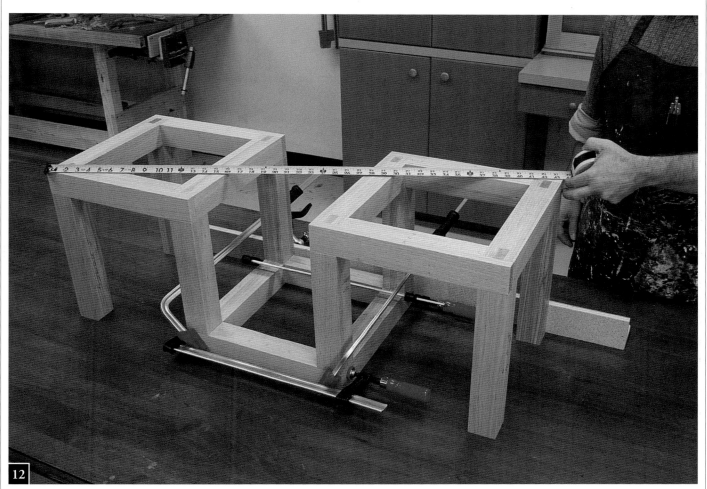

Check the final table assembly for squareness by measuring the diagonals of the coffee table. If the two measurements are equal, the table is square. Adjust the clamp angles if the table needs to be squared up. Note the use of a straight jig to help align the table while clamping. Also, as you will notice, two possible variations are shown for this project. You may simply order glass to fit, and place it on top of your finished coffee table. Or, if you prefer the inset-glass look (as shown on page 36), small oak supports ($\frac{1}{2}$" x $\frac{1}{2}$") can be cut to fit and pinned inside. The glass inserts will rest on those supports.

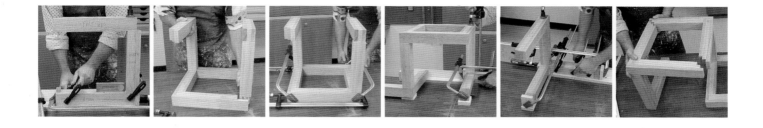

EVOLUTION
coffee table

This is an original design that measures 15" high by 15"

wide by 40½" long. A variation on the Tri-Cube Table

with only four legs with feet, it is moderately easy to

build. It is made of red oak with a clear finish.

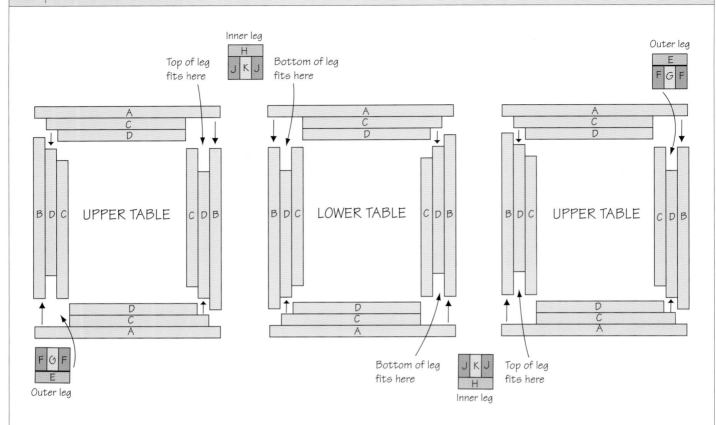

Inner leg

Top of leg fits here

Bottom of leg fits here

Outer leg

UPPER TABLE

LOWER TABLE

UPPER TABLE

Outer leg

Bottom of leg fits here

Top of leg fits here

Inner leg

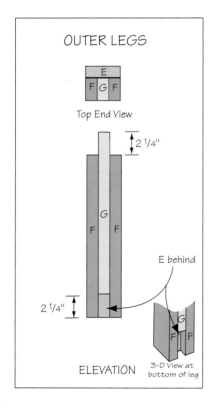

OUTER LEGS

Top End View

2 1/4"

E behind

2 1/4"

ELEVATION

3-D View at bottom of leg

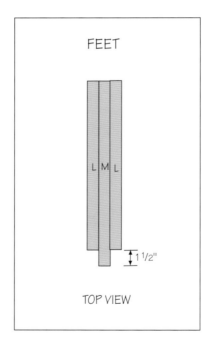

FEET

1 1/2"

TOP VIEW

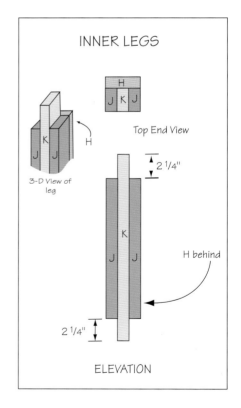

INNER LEGS

3-D View of leg

Top End View

2 1/4"

H behind

2 1/4"

ELEVATION

[CUTTING LIST] *Evolution Coffee Table*

REF.	QTY.	PART	MATERIAL	THICK	WIDTH	LENGTH	COMMENTS
A	6	Tables	Red Oak	$3/4$	$2\frac{1}{4}$	15	
B	6	Tables	Red Oak	$3/4$	$2\frac{1}{4}$	$13\frac{1}{2}$	
C	12	Tables	Red Oak	$3/4$	$2\frac{1}{4}$	12	
D	12	Tables	Red Oak	$3/4$	$2\frac{1}{4}$	$11\frac{1}{4}$	
E	2	Outer Legs	Red Oak	$3/4$	$2\frac{1}{4}$	$12\frac{3}{4}$	
F	4	Outer Legs	Red Oak	$3/4$	$1\frac{1}{2}$	$12\frac{3}{4}$	
G	2	Outer Legs	Red Oak	$3/4$	$1\frac{1}{2}$	$12\frac{3}{4}$	
H	2	Inner Legs	Red Oak	$3/4$	$2\frac{1}{4}$	$10\frac{1}{2}$	
J	4	Inner Legs	Red Oak	$3/4$	$1\frac{1}{2}$	$10\frac{1}{2}$	
K	2	Inner Legs	Red Oak	$3/4$	$1\frac{1}{2}$	15	
L	4	Feet	Red Oak	$3/4$	$2\frac{1}{4}$	$12\frac{3}{4}$	
M	2	Feet	Red Oak	$3/4$	$2\frac{1}{4}$	$14\frac{1}{4}$	

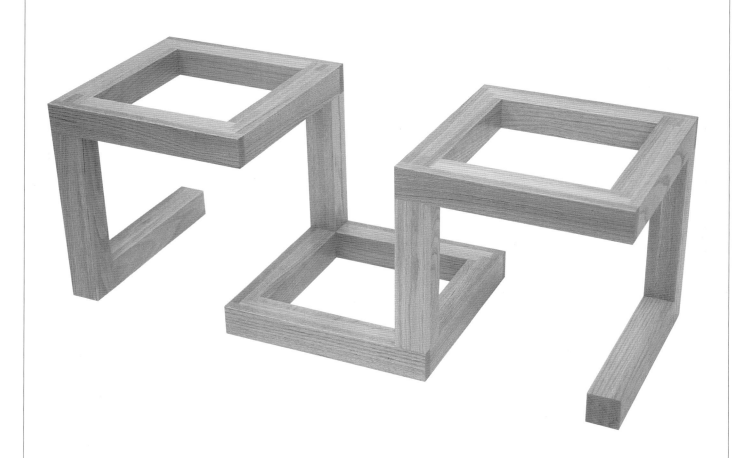

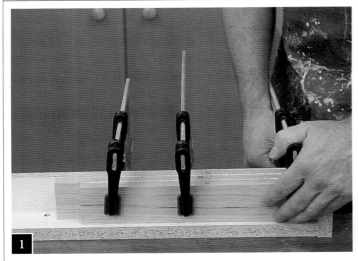

1

Glue-up of LML outer feet. Two (2) of these feet are needed.

2

Assembly of LML foot and EFFG outer leg. The outer leg pieces are glued up at this time because it is easier to capture the foot tenon in the loose parts. Two (2) assemblies are needed.

3

Inner leg HJJK has single-board tenons on both ends.

4

Use the 2¼" spacer to glue up leg HJJK.

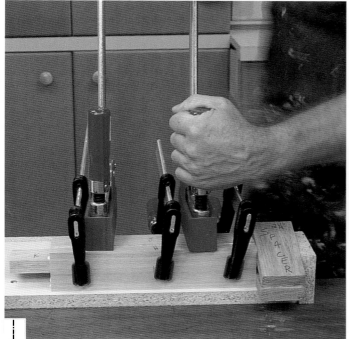

Final clamping of leg HJJK. (Note the vertical clamping. Pressure from two directions is important.) Two (2) inner legs are needed.

Glue-up of inner leg HJJK to foot BDC. (Note the use of clamping blocks at the end of the foot. These help even out the clamping pressure.) Two (2) of these assemblies are needed.

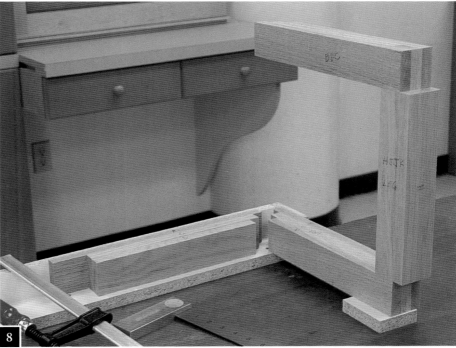

Leg/foot assembly HJJK/BDC is glued to apron BDC. (Note the use of a square. This tool will be used throughout all of these projects. It is very important that all joints be square. This will make later assemblies that much easier to keep square.)

Setup for gluing foot ACD to inner leg/foot/apron assembly. Two (2) of these assemblies are needed.

Final clamping of inner leg/foot/apron assembly to foot ACD.

Glue-up of outer leg/foot assembly EFFG/LML to apron BDC.

Setup for assembly of two inner leg assemblies.

Apply glue to all surfaces of the joint that will touch.

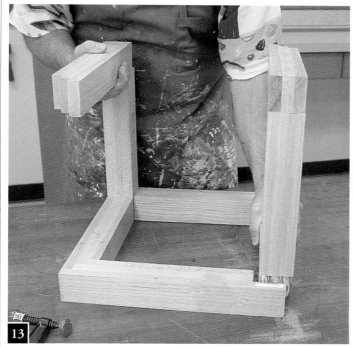

Putting the assemblies together.

Final clamping of the inner table assembly.

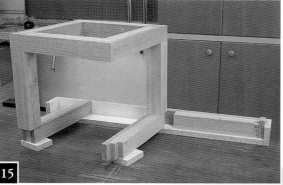

Setup for gluing side apron ACD to inner table assembly.

Clamp the inner assembly to the side apron ACD.

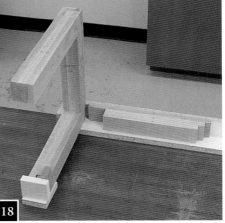

18

Setup for assembly of apron ACD to outer leg assembly.

17

Clamp the other side apron to the inner assembly using the same jig as in photo 16.

Setup for gluing end apron ACD to outer leg/foot/apron assembly.

19

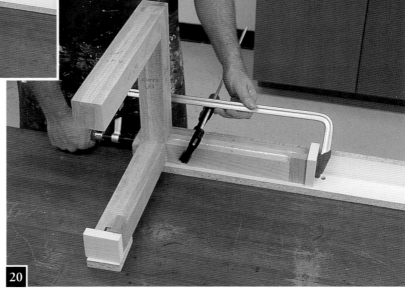

20

Glue up the end apron ACD at the same time it is glued to the outer leg assembly.

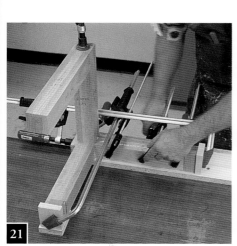

Final clamping of the outer leg assembly. Two (2) of these are needed.

Setup for final assembly of the Evolution Coffee Table.

Final clamping of the outer leg assemblies to the end apron ACD.

three diamonds
COFFEE TABLE

An original design that measures 17" wide by 44⅝" long

by 16" high, this table is a nice variation of the Tri-Cube

Table. The top shown on the project here is only one

possibility. A large oval piece of glass or a rectangular

piece with all four corners clipped are other possibili-

ties. With all parts labeled, it is only moderately difficult

to assemble. The base is made of red oak with a clear

finish. The top shown here is made of MDF that has

been painted and topcoated with clear lacquer.

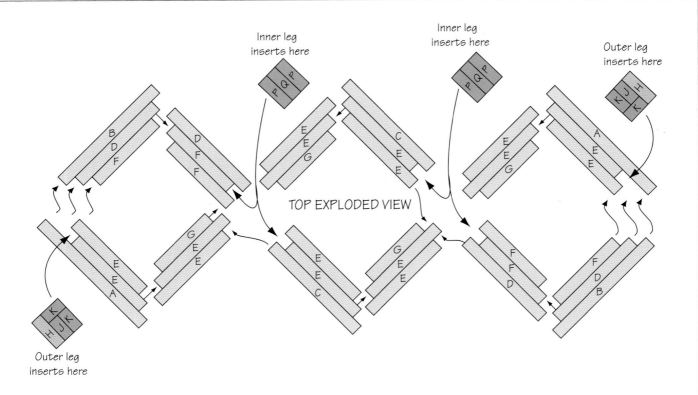

Inner leg inserts here

Inner leg inserts here

Outer leg inserts here

TOP EXPLODED VIEW

Outer leg inserts here

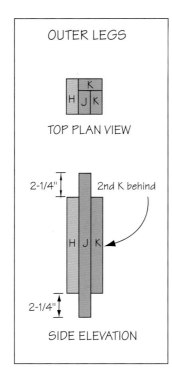

OUTER LEGS

TOP PLAN VIEW

2-1/4" 2nd K behind

2-1/4"

SIDE ELEVATION

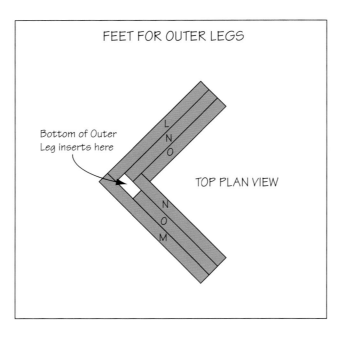

FEET FOR OUTER LEGS

Bottom of Outer Leg inserts here

TOP PLAN VIEW

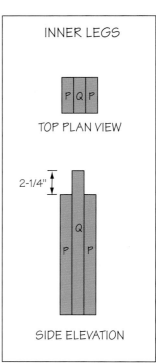

INNER LEGS

TOP PLAN VIEW

2-1/4"

SIDE ELEVATION

[CUTTING LIST] *Three Diamonds Coffee Table*

REF.	QTY.	PART	MATERIAL	THICK	WIDTH	LENGTH	COMMENTS
A	2	Tables	Red Oak	$3/4$	$2\,1/4$	$12\,1/2$	
B	2	Tables	Red Oak	$3/4$	$2\,1/4$	$11\,3/4$	
C	2	Tables	Red Oak	$3/4$	$2\,1/4$	11	
D	4	Tables	Red Oak	$3/4$	$2\,1/4$	$10\,1/4$	
E	16	Tables	Red Oak	$3/4$	$2\,1/4$	$9\,1/2$	
F	6	Tables	Red Oak	$3/4$	$2\,1/4$	$8\,3/4$	
G	4	Tables	Red Oak	$3/4$	$2\,1/4$	8	
H	2	Outer Legs	Red Oak	$3/4$	$2\,1/4$	$11\,1/2$	
J	2	Outer Legs	Red Oak	$3/4$	$1\,1/2$	16	
K	4	Outer Legs	Red Oak	$3/4$	$1\,1/2$	$11\,1/2$	
L	2	Feet	Red Oak	$3/4$	$2\,1/4$	$11\,3/4$	
M	2	Feet	Red Oak	$3/4$	$2\,1/4$	$12\,1/2$	
N	4	Feet	Red Oak	$3/4$	$2\,1/4$	11	
O	4	Feet	Red Oak	$3/4$	$2\,1/4$	$10\,1/4$	
P	4	Inner Legs	Red Oak	$3/4$	$2\,1/4$	$13\,3/4$	
Q	2	Inner Legs	Red Oak	$3/4$	$2\,1/4$	16	

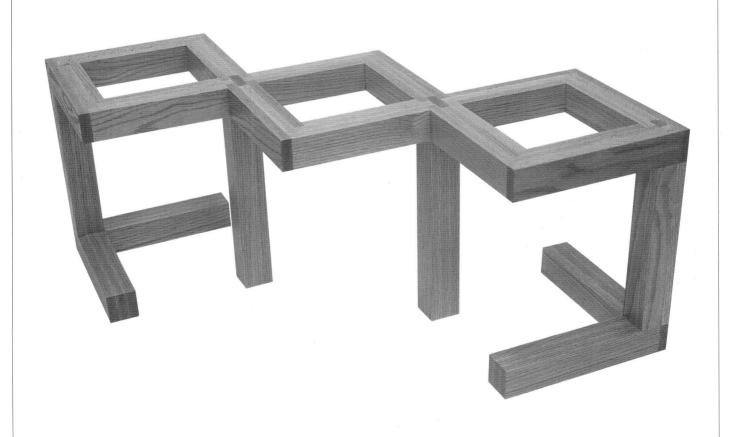

Glue-up of outer leg HJKK. Two (2) are needed.

Glue-up of inner leg PQP. Two (2) are needed.

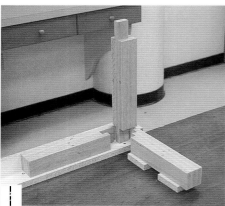

Setup for assembly of foot LNO and foot NOM to outer leg HJKK. Note that both foot assemblies are loose until glue-up.

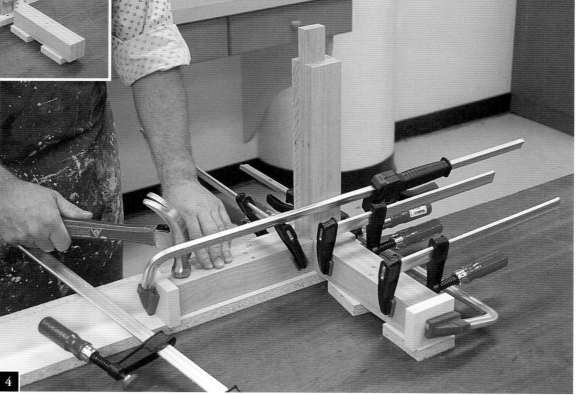

Final glue-up of outer leg/foot assembly.

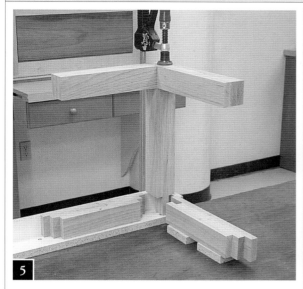

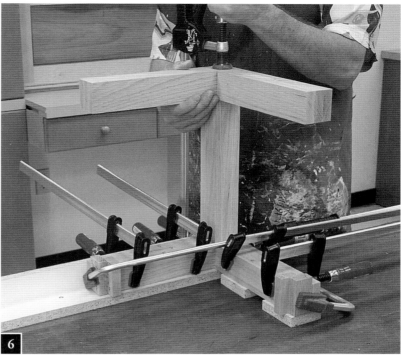

Setup for outer leg/foot assembly to outer aprons AEE and BDF. Aprons are loose until glue-up.

Final glue-up of outer leg/foot assembly to outer aprons. Two (2) of these assemblies are needed.

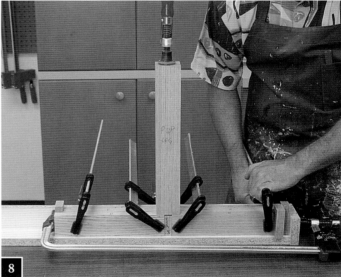

Setup for assembly of leg PQP to rails GEE and GEE. (Note the use of a ¾" spacer where the two rails come together at the leg.)

Final glue-up of leg PCP and two (2) GEE rails. (Note the use of spacers at the ends of the rails. These help even out the clamping pressure.)

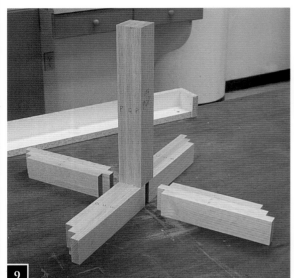

9

10

Photos 9 through 19 show the step-by-step glue-up process. Photo 9 shows set-up for gluing top aprons DFF and CEE to leg PQP assembly. Two (2) of these are needed. Photos 10 and 11 show glue-up of center pieces E and F first.

11

Photos 12 through 19 show glue-up of remaining apron pieces.

12

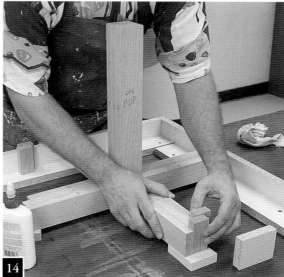

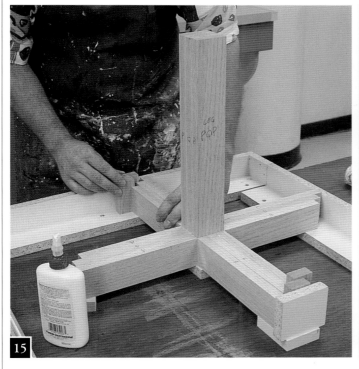

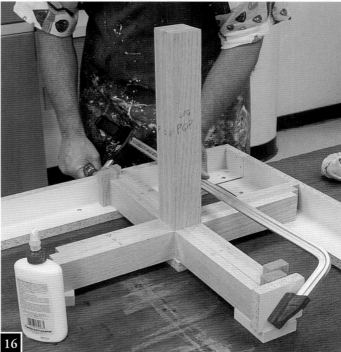

17

18

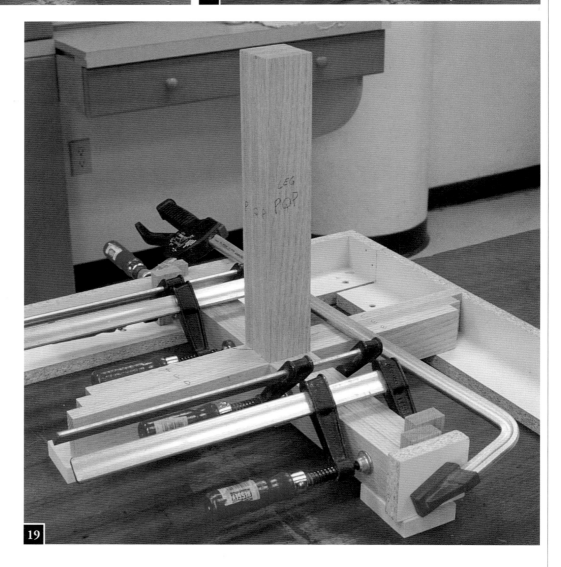

19

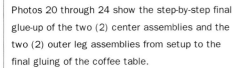

Photos 20 through 24 show the step-by-step final glue-up of the two (2) center assemblies and the two (2) outer leg assemblies from setup to the final gluing of the coffee table.

   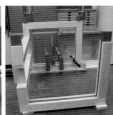 

END
table

An original, this table measures 27" long by 18" wide by 21" high. The design has no beginning and no end. It creates an illusion of the wood twisting and turning so your eye naturally follows the form all around the table. Construction is easy to moderately difficult. This project is made of hard maple and red heart with a clear finish.

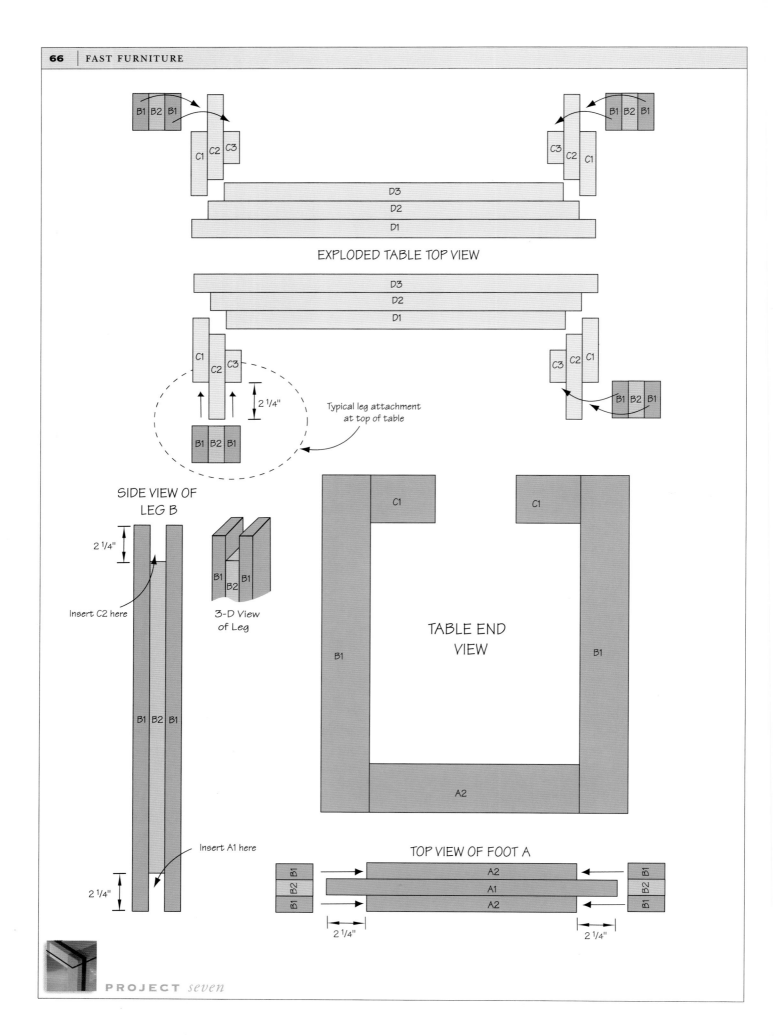

EXPLODED TABLE TOP VIEW

2 1/4"

Typical leg attachment
at top of table

SIDE VIEW OF
LEG B

2 1/4"

Insert C2 here

3-D View
of Leg

Insert A1 here

2 1/4"

TABLE END
VIEW

TOP VIEW OF FOOT A

2 1/4"

2 1/4"

[CUTTING LIST] *End Table*

REF.	QTY.	PART	MATERIAL	THICK	WIDTH	LENGTH	COMMENTS
A1	2	Floor Bar	Red Heart	$3/4$	$2^{1}/_{4}$	18	
A2	4	Floor Bar	Hard Maple	$3/4$	$2^{1}/_{4}$	$13^{1}/_{2}$	
B1	8	Upright Legs	Hard Maple	$3/4$	$2^{1}/_{4}$	21	
B2	4	Upright Legs	Red Heart	$3/4$	$2^{1}/_{4}$	$16^{1}/_{2}$	
C1	4	Short Cross Bars	Hard Maple	$3/4$	$2^{1}/_{4}$	$3^{3}/_{4}$	
C2	4	Short Cross Bars	Red Heart	$3/4$	$2^{1}/_{4}$	$5^{1}/_{4}$	
C3	4	Short Cross Bars	Hard Maple	$3/4$	$2^{1}/_{4}$	$2^{1}/_{4}$	
D1	2	Long Top Bars	Hard Maple	$3/4$	$2^{1}/_{4}$	$25^{1}/_{2}$	
D2	2	Long Top Bars	Red Heart	$3/4$	$2^{1}/_{4}$	24	
D3	2	Long Top Bars	Hard Maple	$3/4$	$2^{1}/_{4}$	$22^{1}/_{2}$	

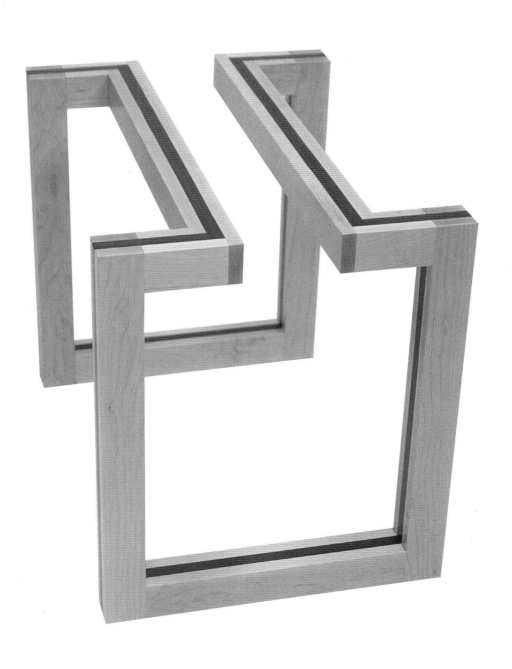

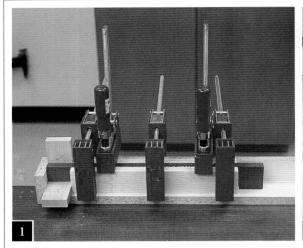

Use the 2¼" spacer to help glue up the foot A1A2A2. Two (2) of these feet are needed.

Glue up the top assembly C1C2C3 and two (2) D1D2D3. Two (2) of these assemblies are needed. All the pieces can be glued together at the same time. This helps to ensure the step-miter joints fit tightly together.

The top assembly C1C2C3 and D1D2D3 and the foot assembly A1A2A2 can be glued to the leg assembly B1B2B1 at the same time. Note the use of a spacer to level the top assembly to the main gluing jig. Two (2) of these top/leg/foot assemblies are needed.

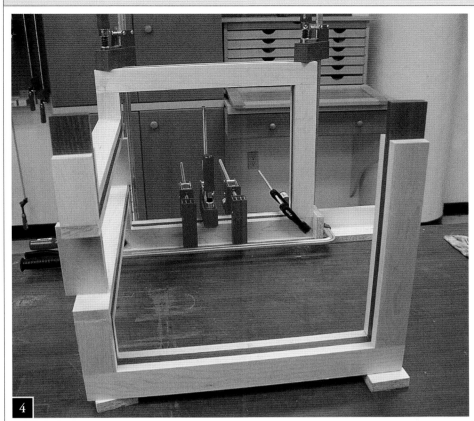

Glue the two (2) top/leg/foot assemblies to a leg B1B2B1. (Prior to glue-up, all the B1B2B1 leg assemblies are loose pieces.) Note spacer to keep top rails aligned.

Attach the final leg assembly B1B2B1 to the table assembly. (Note the spacer used in the final leg glue-ups to keep the top assemblies properly aligned with each other.)

Other Display Options

[ORIGINAL]

[OPTION 1]

[OPTION 2]

[OPTION 3]

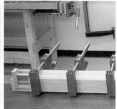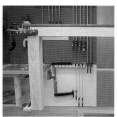

DINING *table*

This dining table measures 36" wide by 60" long by 28½"

high and will seat six people. This is an original design

due to the method of construction. A ½" glass top gives

this table a very light appearance and sleek look. It is

moderately difficult to construct. The project here is

made of ash and has been lacquered black, which lends

to its formal, yet simple, appearance.

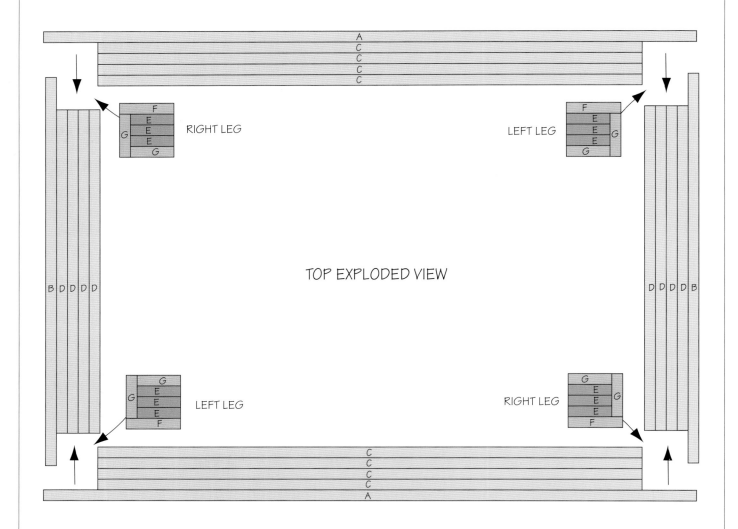

TOP EXPLODED VIEW

A
C
C
C

RIGHT LEG

LEFT LEG

B D D D D

D D D D B

LEFT LEG

RIGHT LEG

C
C
C
A

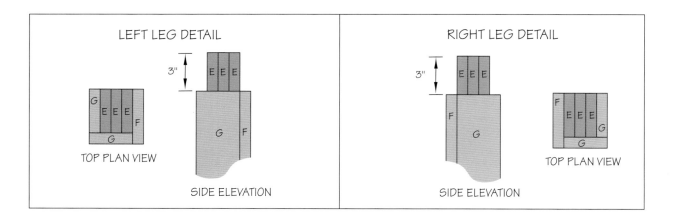

LEFT LEG DETAIL

3"

TOP PLAN VIEW

SIDE ELEVATION

RIGHT LEG DETAIL

3"

TOP PLAN VIEW

SIDE ELEVATION

[CUTTING LIST] *Dining Table*

REF.	QTY.	PART	MATERIAL	THICK	WIDTH	LENGTH	COMMENTS
A	2	Top	Ash	$3/4$	3	60	
B	2	Top	Ash	$3/4$	3	$34^{1}/_{2}$	
C	8	Top	Ash	$3/4$	3	$52^{1}/_{2}$	
D	8	Top	Ash	$3/4$	3	30	
E	12	Legs	Ash	$3/4$	3	$28^{1}/_{2}$	
F	4	Legs	Ash	$3/4$	$3^{3}/_{4}$	$25^{1}/_{2}$	
G	8	Legs	Ash	$3/4$	3	$25^{1}/_{2}$	

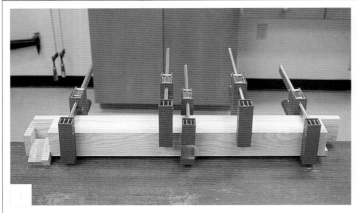

Glue up end rail DDDDB using a 2¼" spacer. Two (2) end rails are needed.

Use a 3" spacer to glue up the side rail CCCCA. Two (2) side rails are needed.

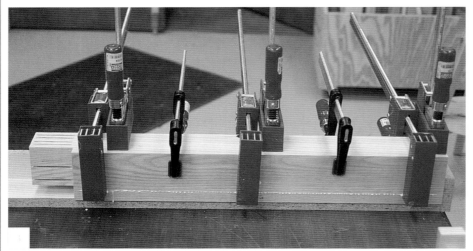

Glue up leg EEEGG. To make the end grain of the legs consistent at final table assembly, make two (2) right legs and two (2) left legs.

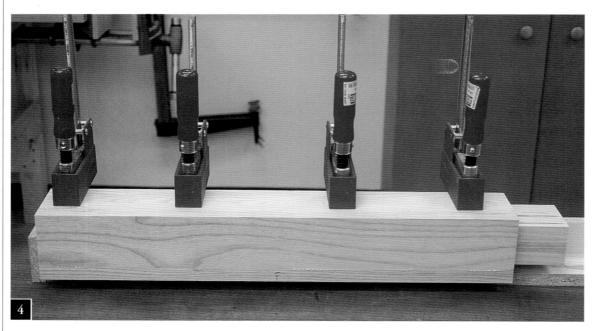

Add F to the EEEGG leg assembly. (Remember to make two [2] right and two [2] left legs.)

PROJECT *eight*

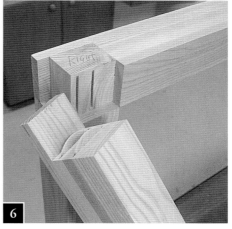

For added strength on this large dining table, biscuits may be added to the corner joints.

Glue up side rail CCCCA and a right and left leg. Two (2) of these side assemblies are needed.

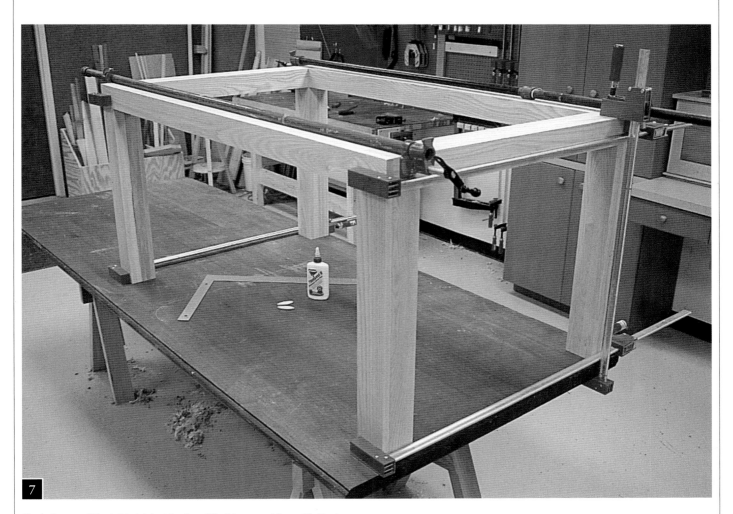

Final glue-up of the table joining the two (2) side assemblies with the two (2) end rails. (Note the use of clamps at the feet of the table. This helps to keep all the legs square until the glue sets up.)

STEP
table

This table is 16" wide by 26" long by 26" high. It functions well as an end table or night stand. The two glass tops keep the look clean and simple but still provide surface. This table is moderately difficult to build and is made of sugar pine with a clear finish.

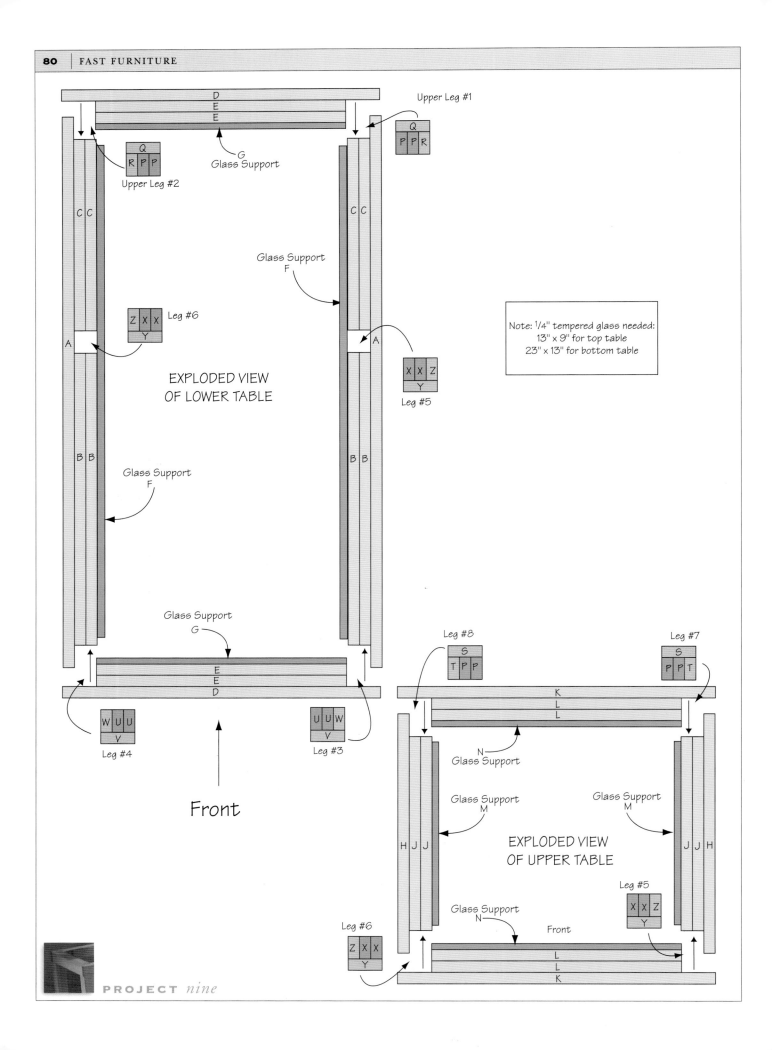

Upper Leg #1

G
Glass Support

Upper Leg #2

Glass Support
F

Leg #6

Note: 1/4" tempered glass needed:
13" x 9" for top table
23" x 13" for bottom table

EXPLODED VIEW
OF LOWER TABLE

Leg #5

Glass Support
F

Glass Support
G

Leg #4

Leg #3

Front

Leg #8

Leg #7

K

Glass Support
N

Glass Support
M

Glass Support
M

EXPLODED VIEW
OF UPPER TABLE

Leg #5

Leg #6

Glass Support
N

Front

K | H | K

S | T

Legs 7R-8L

Z | Y

Legs 5R-6L

← Front

D | A | D

Q | R

Legs
1R-2L

W | V

Legs
3R-4L

LEG DETAILS

LEG 1	LEG 2	LEG 3	LEG 4

LEG 1
P
P | Q
R

LEG 2
P
Q | P
R

LEG 3
U
V | U
W

LEG 4
U
U | V
W

Top Views

P

R | Q

P

Q | R

U

V | W

U

W | V

Elevations

LEG 5	LEG 6	LEG 7	LEG 8

LEG 5
X
Y | X
Z

LEG 6
X
X | Y
Z

LEG 7
P
P | S
T

LEG 8
P
S | P
T

Top Views

X

Y | Z

X

Z | Y

P

T | S

P

S | T

Elevations

[CUTTING LIST] *Step Table*

REF.	QTY.	PART	MATERIAL	THICK	WIDTH	LENGTH	COMMENTS
A	2	Bottom	Sugar Pine	$\frac{1}{2}$	$1\frac{1}{2}$	25	
B	4	Bottom	Sugar Pine	$\frac{1}{2}$	$1\frac{1}{2}$	13	
C	4	Bottom	Sugar Pine	$\frac{1}{2}$	$1\frac{1}{2}$	9	
D	2	Bottom	Sugar Pine	$\frac{1}{2}$	$1\frac{1}{2}$	16	
E	4	Bottom	Sugar Pine	$\frac{1}{2}$	$1\frac{1}{2}$	13	
F	2	Glass Top Support	Sugar Pine	$\frac{1}{4}$	$1\frac{1}{4}$	$22\frac{1}{2}$	
G	2	Glass Top Support	Sugar Pine	$\frac{1}{4}$	$1\frac{1}{4}$	13	

TOP TABLE

REF.	QTY.	PART	MATERIAL	THICK	WIDTH	LENGTH	COMMENTS
H	2	Top	Sugar Pine	$\frac{1}{2}$	$1\frac{1}{2}$	11	
J	4	Top	Sugar Pine	$\frac{1}{2}$	$1\frac{1}{2}$	9	
K	2	Top	Sugar Pine	$\frac{1}{2}$	$1\frac{1}{2}$	16	
L	4	Top	Sugar Pine	$\frac{1}{2}$	$1\frac{1}{2}$	13	
M	2	Glass Top Support	Sugar Pine	$\frac{1}{4}$	$1\frac{1}{4}$	$8\frac{1}{2}$	
N	2	Glass Top Support	Sugar Pine	$\frac{1}{4}$	$1\frac{1}{4}$	13	

LEGS

REF.	QTY.	PART	MATERIAL	THICK	WIDTH	LENGTH	COMMENTS
P	4	Legs	Sugar Pine	$\frac{1}{2}$	1	26	For legs 1, 2, 7, 8
Q	2	Legs	Sugar Pine	$\frac{1}{2}$	$1\frac{1}{2}$	$14\frac{1}{2}$	For legs 1, 2
R	2	Legs	Sugar Pine	$\frac{1}{2}$	1	$14\frac{1}{2}$	For legs 1, 2
S	2	Legs	Sugar Pine	$\frac{1}{2}$	$1\frac{1}{2}$	$8\frac{1}{2}$	For legs 7, 8
T	2	Legs	Sugar Pine	$\frac{1}{2}$	1	$8\frac{1}{2}$	For legs 7, 8
U	4	Legs	Sugar Pine	$\frac{1}{2}$	1	16	For legs 3, 4
V	2	Legs	Sugar Pine	$\frac{1}{2}$	$1\frac{1}{2}$	$14\frac{1}{2}$	For legs 3, 4
W	2	Legs	Sugar Pine	$\frac{1}{2}$	1	$14\frac{1}{2}$	For legs 3, 4
X	4	Legs	Sugar Pine	$\frac{1}{2}$	1	$11\frac{1}{2}$	For legs 5, 6
Y	2	Legs	Sugar Pine	$\frac{1}{2}$	$1\frac{1}{2}$	$8\frac{1}{2}$	For legs 5, 6
Z	2	Legs	Sugar Pine	$\frac{1}{2}$	1	$8\frac{1}{2}$	For legs 5, 6

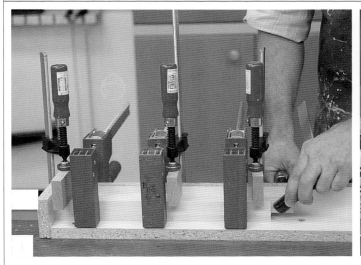

Glue up front legs UUVW, 3 and 4. (When gluing up the legs for this table, double-check the illustrations to be sure of the configuration of all the leg parts.)

Use 1½" spacers to glue up upper center legs XXYZ, 5 and 6.

Glue up the front sides of the lower apron ABB using a 1" spacer.

Glue up apron ABB to front leg UUVW. Make left and right assemblies.

Assemble the lower rear legs PPQR, 1 and 2.

6

7

Attach upper center leg XXYZ to the side apron assembly. Make left and right assemblies. Both side assemblies are easily assembled using the bench vise.

Glue up the side rear apron pieces CC to the side assemblies. Left and right assemblies are needed.

8

Attach the lower rear leg assembly PPQR to the side apron assembly. Again, left and right assemblies are needed.

9

Glue up upper side apron HJJ using a 1" spacer. (This same technique is used to glue up lower front and back aprons DEE and upper front and back aprons KLL. Aprons DEE and KLL are glued up using a 1½" spacer.)

10

Attach the two (2) side assemblies together using the lower front and rear aprons DEE.

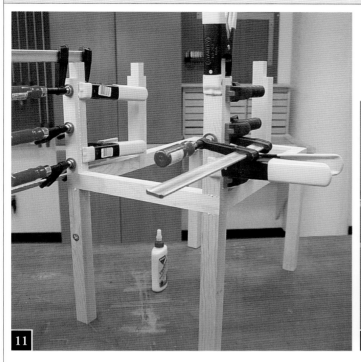

Glue the two (2) leg pieces S and T to the rear upper legs creating legs 7 and 8.

Glue the two (2) upper side aprons to the table assembly.

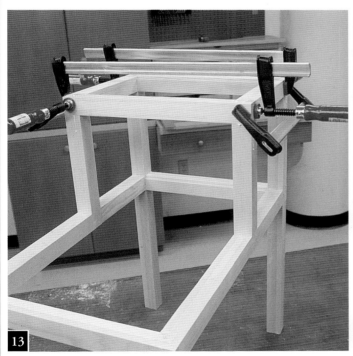

Attach the two (2) upper front and back aprons KLL to the table assembly.

Attach the long glass supports F and N, then attach the shorter glass supports G and M.

Detail of installed glass supports.

the "**X**" table

This original table has strength, utility and simplicity of design. It is sturdy and can function as an end table or a small coffee table. Construction is easy to moderately difficult. This project is made of red oak with a clear finish.

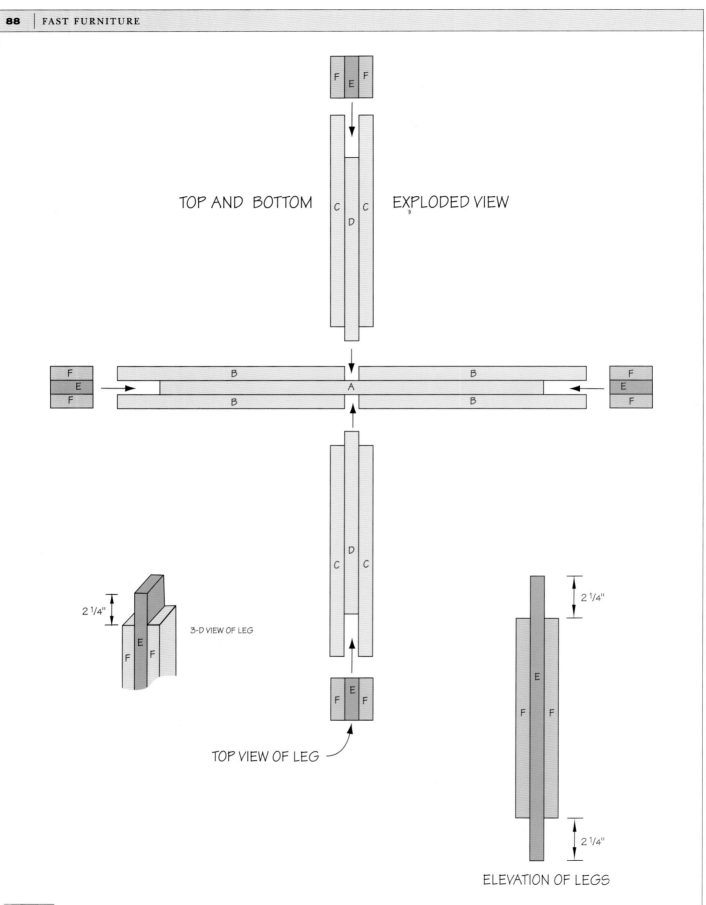

TOP AND BOTTOM   EXPLODED VIEW

3-D VIEW OF LEG

TOP VIEW OF LEG

ELEVATION OF LEGS

2 1/4"

2 1/4"

2 1/4"

[CUTTING LIST] *The "X" Table*

REF.	QTY.	PART	MATERIAL	THICK	WIDTH	LENGTH	COMMENTS
A	2	Top/Bottom	Red Oak	3/4	2 1/4	19 1/2	
B	8	Top/Bottom	Red Oak	3/4	2 1/4	11 5/8	
C	8	Top/Bottom	Red Oak	3/4	2 1/4	10 7/8	
D	4	Top/Bottom	Red Oak	3/4	2 1/4	9 3/8	
E	4	Legs	Red Oak	3/4	2 1/4	15	
F	8	Legs	Red Oak	3/4	2 1/4	10 1/2	

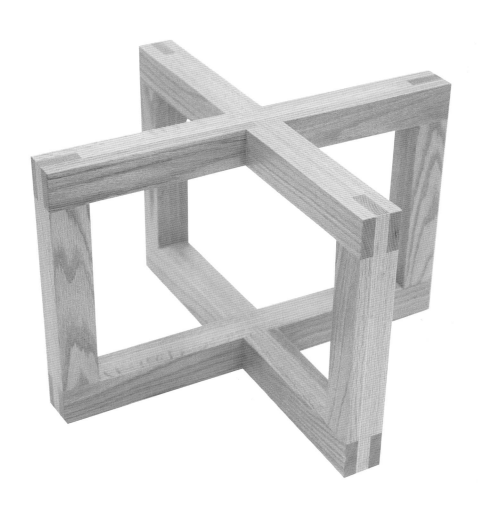

Glue-up of leg FEF and two (2) CDC stretcher assemblies. Two (2) of these assemblies are needed. Two (2) individual legs FEF are also needed. These are glued up using a 2¼" spacer. These legs have a single tenon on each end.

Make the center assembly by gluing up two (2) rails BAB and two (2) FEF legs. (Note the ¾" spacer in the center on the BBABB rail. This creates the mortise for the CDC stretcher tenons to fit into.)

Final glue-up of the table using the two (2) stretcher assemblies FEF, CDC, CDC and the center assembly. (Note the clamp across the legs. This may be used to help square the unit if necessary.)

Other Possible Sizes

As with any of the projects in this book, you can alter dimensions to fit just about any need. For example, take a look at the two extra cutting lists shown below. These lists show how to alter the dimensions to make two smaller tables — one from ½" wood, and one from ¼". When the longest dimension of a table is 12" down to 8", ½" stock is recommended. From 8" down to 6", ¼" stock is recommended. By using stock of a smaller dimension, the tables won't look as chunky or heavy as they would if thicker stock was used.

[CUTTING LIST] *Smaller "X" Table*

REF.	QTY.	PART	MATERIAL	THICK	WIDTH	LENGTH	COMMENTS
A	2	Top/Bottom	Red Oak	½	1½	13	
B	8	Top/Bottom	Red Oak	½	1½	7¾	
C	8	Top/Bottom	Red Oak	½	1½	7¼	
D	4	Top/Bottom	Red Oak	½	1½	6¼	
E	4	Legs	Red Oak	½	1½	10	
F	8	Legs	Red Oak	½	1½	7	

[CUTTING LIST] *Smallest "X" Table*

REF.	QTY.	PART	MATERIAL	THICK	WIDTH	LENGTH	COMMENTS
A	2	Top/Bottom	Red Oak	¼	¾	6½	
B	8	Top/Bottom	Red Oak	¼	¾	3⅞	
C	8	Top/Bottom	Red Oak	¼	¾	3⅝	
D	4	Top/Bottom	Red Oak	¼	¾	3⅛	
E	4	Legs	Red Oak	¼	¾	5	
F	8	Legs	Red Oak	¼	¾	3½	

bedspread VALET

This project could also be used as a quilt stand or towel rack. It is 30" high with a 30"-long top bar. The base is 11¼" wide and 18" long. This is a moderately difficult project to build, made of red oak with a clear finish.

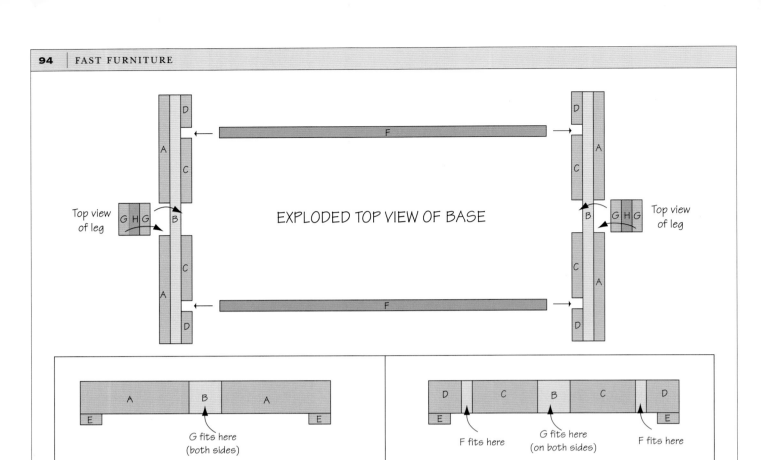

EXPLODED TOP VIEW OF BASE

Top view of leg

Top view of leg

OUTER ELEVATION OF BASE

G fits here (both sides)

INNER ELEVATION OF BASE

F fits here

G fits here (on both sides)

F fits here

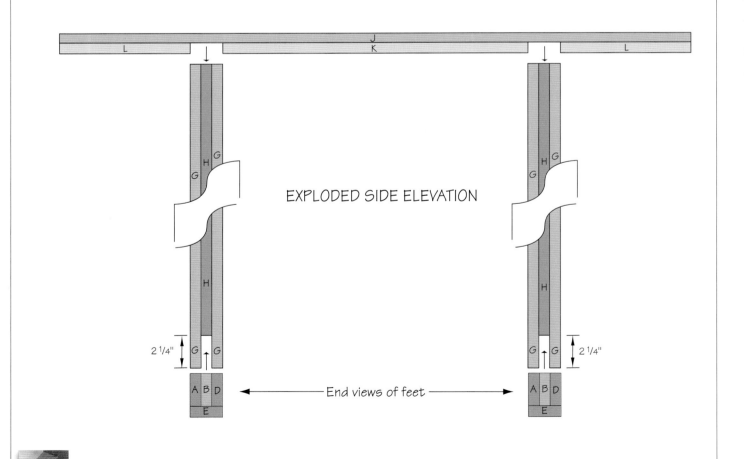

EXPLODED SIDE ELEVATION

2 1/4"

2 1/4"

End views of feet

[CUTTING LIST] *Bedspread Valet*

REF.	QTY.	PART	MATERIAL	THICK	WIDTH	LENGTH	COMMENTS
A	4	Base	Red Oak	$3/4$	$2^1/4$	$4^1/2$	
B	2	Base	Red Oak	$3/4$	$2^1/4$	$11^1/4$	
C	4	Base	Red Oak	$3/4$	$2^1/4$	$2^1/4$	
D	4	Base	Red Oak	$3/4$	$2^1/4$	$1^1/2$	
E	4	Base	Red Oak	$3/4$	$2^1/4$	$1^1/2$	
F	2	Base	Red Oak	$3/4$	$2^1/4$	15	
G	4	Uprights	Red Oak	$3/4$	$2^1/4$	$28^1/2$	
H	2	Uprights	Red Oak	$3/4$	$2^1/4$	$26^1/4$	
J	1	Top Bar	Red Oak	$3/4$	$2^1/4$	30	
K	1	Top Bar	Red Oak	$3/4$	$2^1/4$	$13^1/2$	
L	2	Top Bar	Red Oak	$3/4$	$2^1/4$	6	

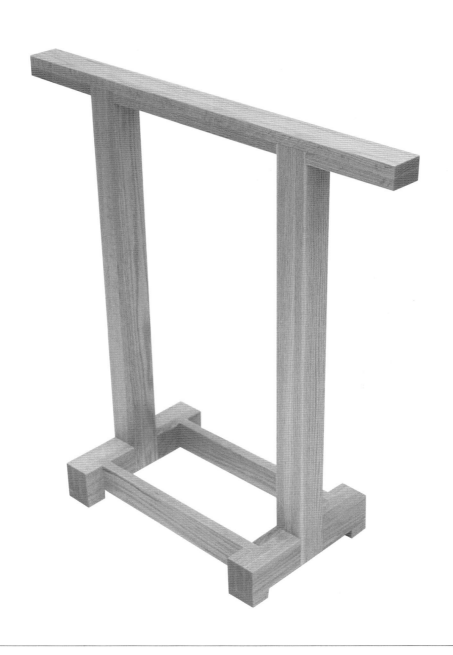

Assemble leg GHG using 2¼" spacer to create the through mortise. Two (2) legs are needed.

Glue up foot AABCC (no D yet) to leg GHG.

The leg will self-center when the two (2) A pieces are put into place with the leg. This whole assembly can be pushed against the jig side for proper alignment. Clamp in the usual way. Two (2) of these assemblies are needed.

The two (2) leg/foot assemblies are connected with two (2) stretchers F. The two (2) D foot pieces are also attached at this time. Lay this assembly out as it will go together. Get all clamps ready, then proceed with the glue-up. (See photos 5 through 7.)

PROJECT *eleven*

Glue-up of valet base to the legs,
shown in photos 5 through 7.

Attach the crossarm pieces JKLL.

The final step is to glue up the four (4) feet E.

greek key DESK

An original, this desk measures 40" long by 18" wide by 28½" high. The design encourages your eyes to follow the Greek key pattern around the entire desk; there is no beginning and no end. The use of contrasting colors of woods enhances the effect of the "movement" of this desk. Construction is moderately easy. This project is made of cherry and walnut with a clear finish.

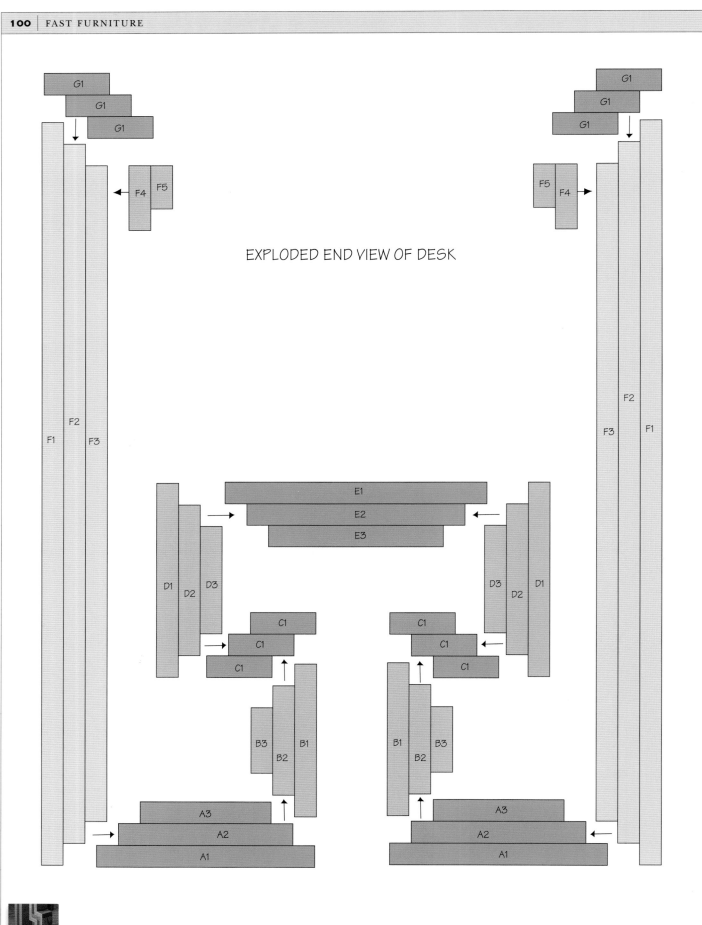

EXPLODED END VIEW OF DESK

[CUTTING LIST] *Greek Key Desk*

REF.	QTY.	PART	MATERIAL	THICK	WIDTH	LENGTH	COMMENTS
A1	4	Base	Cherry	$3/4$	$2^{1}/4$	$7^{1}/2$	
A2	4	Base	Walnut	$3/4$	$2^{1}/4$	6	
A3	4	Base	Cherry	$3/4$	$2^{1}/4$	$4^{1}/2$	
B1	4	Inner Leg	Cherry	$3/4$	$2^{1}/4$	$5^{1}/4$	
B2	4	Inner Leg	Walnut	$3/4$	$2^{1}/4$	$3^{3}/4$	
B3	4	Inner Leg	Cherry	$3/4$	$2^{1}/4$	$2^{1}/4$	
C1	12	Greek Key Bottom	*	$3/4$	$2^{1}/4$	$2^{1}/4$	* Make 4 from walnut, the rest from cherry
D1	4	Greek Key Sides	Cherry	$3/4$	$2^{1}/4$	$6^{3}/4$	
D2	4	Greek Key Sides	Walnut	$3/4$	$2^{1}/4$	$5^{1}/4$	
D3	4	Greek Key Sides	Cherry	$3/4$	$2^{1}/4$	$3^{3}/4$	
E1	2	Greek Key Top	Cherry	$3/4$	$2^{1}/4$	18	
E2	2	Greek Key Top	Walnut	$3/4$	$2^{1}/4$	$16^{1}/2$	
E3	2	Greek Key Top	Cherry	$3/4$	$2^{1}/4$	15	
F1	4	Outer Legs	Cherry	$3/4$	$2^{1}/4$	$27^{3}/4$	
F2	4	Outer Legs	Walnut	$3/4$	$2^{1}/4$	$26^{1}/4$	
F3	4	Outer Legs	Cherry	$3/4$	$2^{1}/4$	$24^{3}/4$	
F4	4	Inner Top Brace	Cherry	$3/4$	$2^{1}/4$	$2^{1}/4$	
F5	4	Outer Top Brace	Walnut	$3/4$	$2^{1}/4$	$1^{1}/2$	
G1	6	Top Runners	*	$3/4$	$2^{1}/4$	48	* Make 2 from walnut, the rest from cherry

Polyurethane glue is highly recommended for gluing up this desk.

Setup for gluing subassembly E1E2E3 and two (2) D1D2D3.
(Note the spacers to level the assembly with the jig.)

By using spacers at the ends of the D parts, clamp pressure
is evened out.

Have clamps ready and begin glue-up.

All parts can have glue applied to them in just a few seconds.

Put the spacers into place.

Clamp the length first.

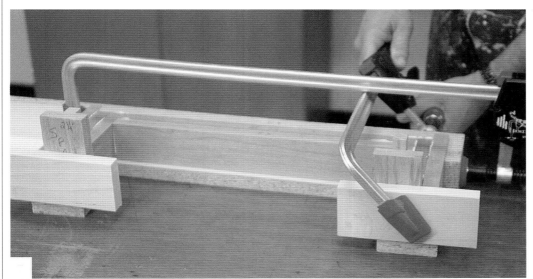

Then pull the D assemblies tight.

Use just enough clamping pressure to pull the joint tight.

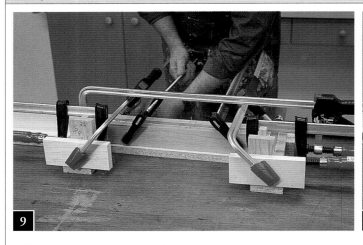

9

Add clamps across the D assemblies.

10

Finally, add clamps across the C assembly.

11

Setup for C1C1C1, B1B2B3,
A1A2A3.

Glue and clamp the
length of the assembly.

12

13

Add clamps across the B assembly.

14

Add clamps across the A assembly.

15

Finally, put a clamp across the joint. Four (4) of these ABC assemblies are needed.

16

Setup for gluing up the three subassemblies.

Clamp the two ABC subassemblies into place on the straight jig. This will keep the whole assembly square.

17

Apply glue to all surfaces of the step-miter joints.

18

Clamp the joint top to bottom.

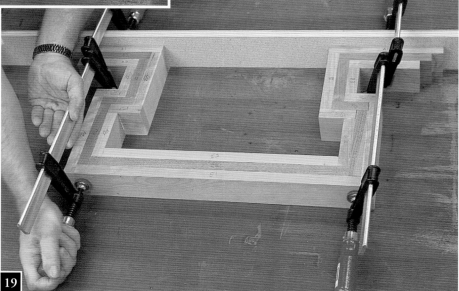

19

PROJECT *twelve*

20

Clamp across the joint. Two (2) of these assemblies are needed.

21

Setup for gluing up the desk end assemblies. (Note the spacer at the tops of the legs.) Apply glue to the peg parts F1F2F3 and to the step-miter joint of the legs and the base subassembly.

22

Using jigs at right angles to each other will help keep the desk end assembly square.

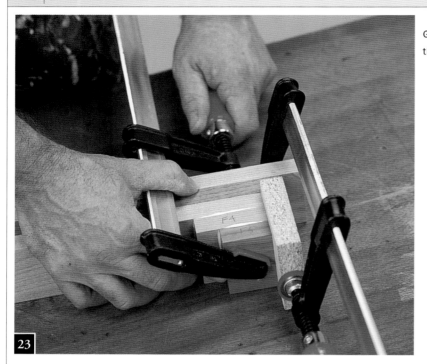

Glue the F4F5 pieces at the top of the legs.

Glue on the G1 rail pieces one at a time.

Make sure the joints at the tops of the legs and the G pieces are tight.

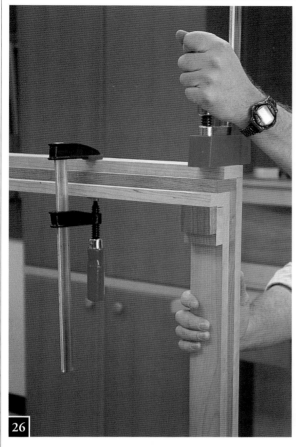

26

Attach the top G rail.

27

Clamp along the whole length of the G rail.

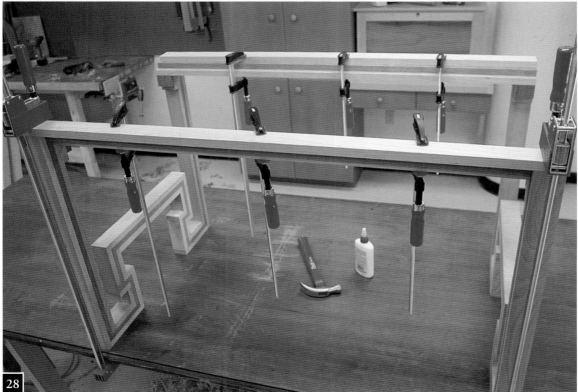

Final desk assembly clamped up. Let the glue cure overnight.

28

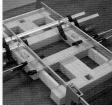

ASIA
table

This table is an original, but the design was inspired by
Asian door handles. Years ago, I was reading a 1930s
National Geographic article about Asia. I saw a photo of
two large metal handles on a pair of glass doors on a
large office building — one half of this design was on
each door. The design was described as the symbol for
the word *Asia*. This table measures 30" long by 18" wide
by 17½" high and is moderately easy to build. This table
is made of red oak and walnut with a clear finish.

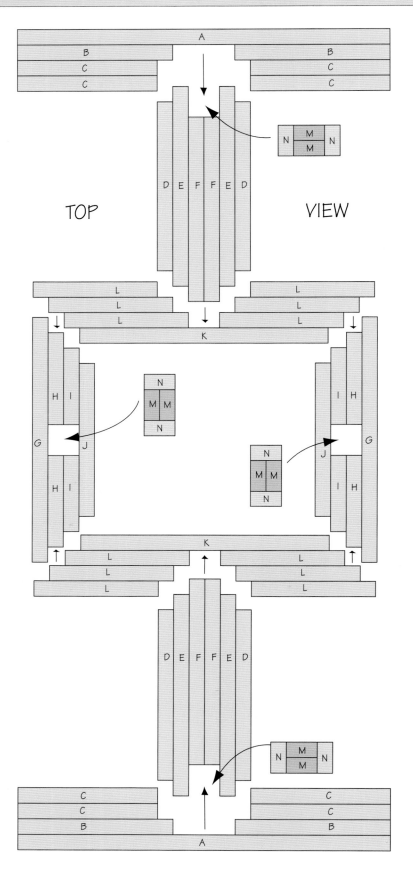

TOP　　　　VIEW

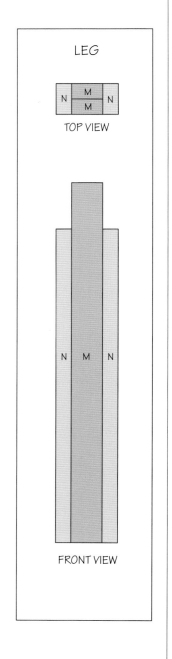

LEG

TOP VIEW

FRONT VIEW

[CUTTING LIST] *Asia Table*

REF.	QTY.	PART	MATERIAL	THICK	WIDTH	LENGTH	COMMENTS
A	2	Ends	Red Oak	$3/4$	$2^1/4$	18	
B	4	Ends	Red Oak	$3/4$	$2^1/4$	$7^1/2$	
C	8	Ends	Red Oak	$3/4$	$2^1/4$	$6^3/4$	
D	4	Connections	Red Oak	$3/4$	$2^1/4$	$8^1/4$	
E	4	Connections	Red Oak	$3/4$	$2^1/4$	$9^3/4$	
F	4	Connections	Red Oak	$3/4$	$2^1/4$	9	
G	2	Center Sides	Red Oak	$3/4$	$2^1/4$	12	
H	4	Center Sides	Red Oak	$3/4$	$2^1/4$	$4^1/2$	
I	4	Center Sides	Red Oak	$3/4$	$2^1/4$	$3^3/4$	
J	2	Center Sides	Red Oak	$3/4$	$2^1/4$	$7^1/2$	
K	2	Center Cross Bars	Red Oak	$3/4$	$2^1/4$	12	
L	12	Center Cross Bars	Red Oak	$3/4$	$2^1/4$	6	
M	8	Legs	Walnut	$3/4$	$1^1/2$	$18^1/4$	
N	8	Legs	Red Oak	$3/4$	$1^1/2$	$15^1/4$	

Glue-up of leg MMNN. Four (4) legs are needed.

Assembly of KLLL and DEFFED. When these parts are glued up at the same time, the step-miter joints are easier to fit together. Two (2) of these assemblies are needed.

Lay out all the top subassemblies and double-check the fit of all the step-miter joints.

Glue-up of assembly KLLL, DEFFED to ABBCCCC. (Note the use of the 1½" spacer to create the through mortise for the leg.) Two (2) of these assemblies are needed.

Final glue-up and clamping of the top. (Note the use of spacers to help keep the top square.) The two (2) GHHIIJ assemblies are loose until final glue-up.

Dry fit the legs for a snug (but not too tight) fit.

Rounding over or "breaking" the top edges of the legs is done easily before final assembly of the table.

Put glue on the inside edges of the tenons on the legs and slide them into the mortises. This will keep the glue from getting all over the top of the tenons on the legs. Clamp squarely and let the glue dry overnight.

Another view of the clamping of the legs.

offset-leg TABLE

This original table is 45" long by 24" wide by 28½" high.

This multipurpose table can be a unique desk, a side-

board or a hall table. Contrasting pieces of wood can be

used to elevate a glass top and give the table a lighter

look. A bottom could be put in the center area and

used to display coins, stamps, silk flowers or whatever

suits your taste. This table is moderately difficult to make

and is made of red oak and red heart with a clear finish.

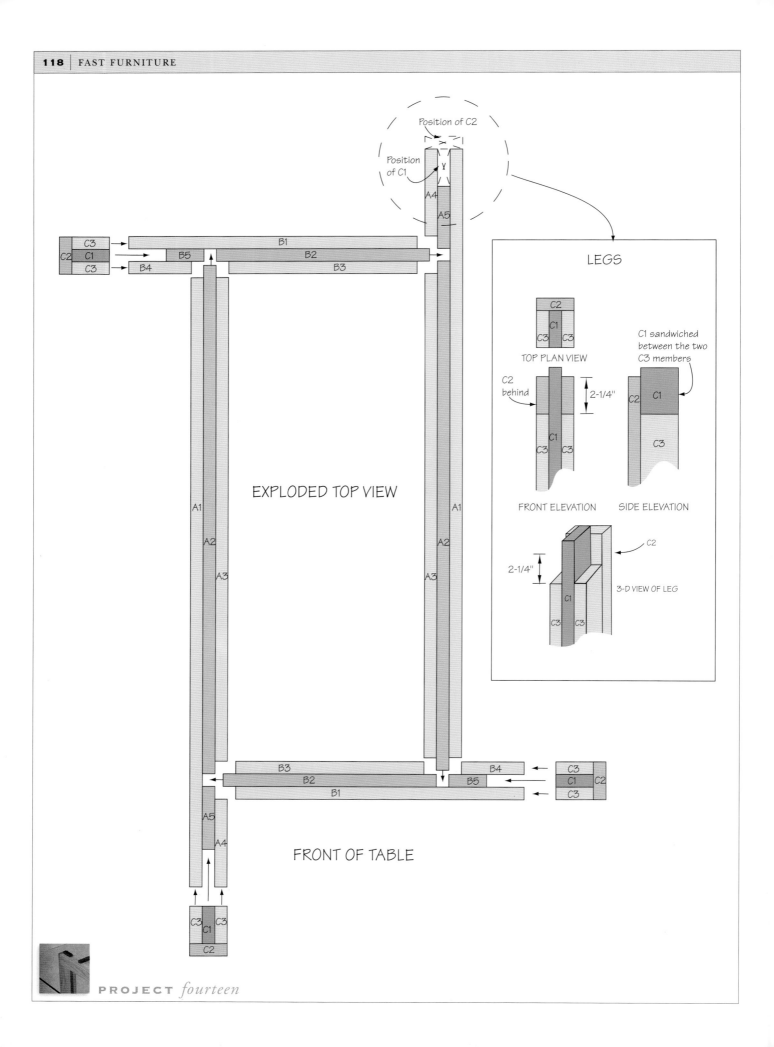

Position of C2

Position of C1

A4

A5

C3

C2 C1

C3

B5

B4

B1

B2

B3

A1

A2

A3

EXPLODED TOP VIEW

A1

A2

A3

LEGS

C2

C1

C3 C3

TOP PLAN VIEW

C2 behind

2-1/4"

C3 C1 C3

FRONT ELEVATION

C1 sandwiched between the two C3 members

C2 C1

C3

SIDE ELEVATION

2-1/4"

C1

C3 C3

C2

3-D VIEW OF LEG

B3

B2

B1

B4

B5

C3

C1 C2

C3

A5

A4

FRONT OF TABLE

C3 C3

C1

C2

[CUTTING LIST] *Offset-Leg Table*

REF.	QTY.	PART	MATERIAL	THICK	WIDTH	LENGTH	COMMENTS
A1	2	Top	Red Oak	$3/4$	$2^{1}/4$	$36^{3}/4$	
A2	2	Top	Red Heart	$3/4$	$2^{3}/4$	$30^{3}/4$	
A3	2	Top	Red Oak	$3/4$	$2^{1}/4$	$29^{1}/4$	
A4	2	Top	Red Oak	$3/4$	$2^{1}/4$	$5^{1}/4$	
A5	2	Top	Red Oak	$3/4$	$2^{1}/4$	$3^{3}/4$	
B1	2	Top	Red Oak	$3/4$	$2^{1}/4$	$17^{1}/4$	
B2	2	Top	Red Oak	$3/4$	$2^{1}/4$	$12^{3}/4$	
B3	2	Top	Red Oak	$3/4$	$2^{1}/4$	$11^{1}/4$	
B4	2	Top	Red Oak	$3/4$	$2^{1}/4$	$3^{3}/4$	
B5	2	Top	Red Oak	$3/4$	$2^{1}/4$	$2^{1}/4$	
C1	4	Legs	Red Heart	$3/4$	$2^{1}/4$	29	
C2	4	Legs	Red Oak	$3/4$	$2^{1}/4$	$28^{1}/2$	
C3	8	Legs	Red Oak	$3/4$	$2^{1}/4$	$26^{1}/4$	

Polyurethane glue is recommended for this project.

1

Glue-up of leg C1C2C3C3. (Note the extension of part C1. This extension will support the glass top and help to give it a "floating" look.)

2

Final clamping of leg.

3

The orientation of the leg to the apron. All the aprons will be similar in assembly.

4

Glue-up of leg and A1A4A5. Gluing these apron parts first is easier than trying to glue up the whole apron at one time.

Apron parts A2 and A3 can now be glued up. (Note the spacers used to create the triple mortise for the apron ends.) All the aprons (A parts and B parts) are glued up in this same manner.

Assemble an end to a side. Two (2) are needed.

Final assembly.

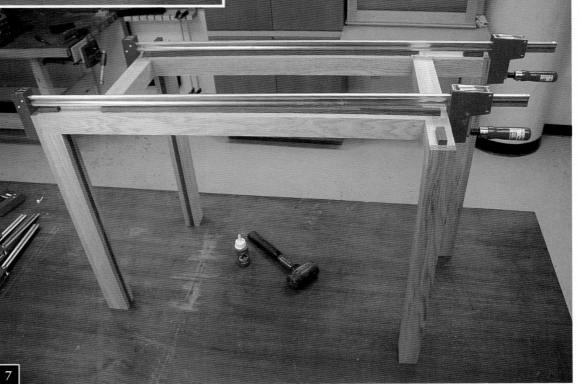

picture/mirror FRAME

Have you ever made a wooden picture frame? I have, using my power equipment, corner clamps, staple gun, brads and other necessary materials. This frame simplifies this whole process and can be made with just clamps and glue. This original frame design has a nice "stair-step" movement that draws your eye in and out of the picture or mirror. It's easy to downsize or upsize the frame to suit your needs. This frame is 18" high by 12" wide and is easy to build. This project is made of red oak with a clear finish.

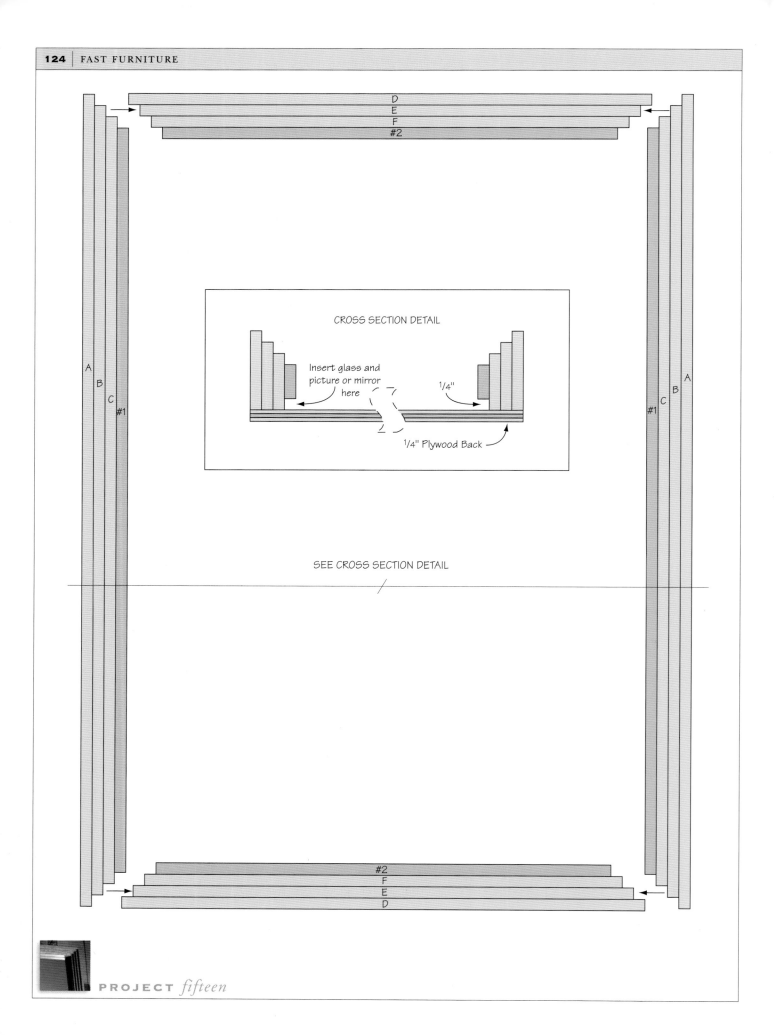

CROSS SECTION DETAIL

Insert glass and
picture or mirror
here

1/4"

1/4" Plywood Back

SEE CROSS SECTION DETAIL

[CUTTING LIST] *Picture/Mirror Frame*

REF.	QTY.	PART	MATERIAL	THICK	WIDTH	LENGTH	COMMENTS
A	2	Sides	Red Oak	$1/4$	$1\,3/4$	18	
B	2	Sides	Red Oak	$1/4$	$1\,1/2$	$17\,1/2$	
C	2	Sides	Red Oak	$1/4$	$1\,1/4$	17	
#1	2	Sides	Red Oak	$1/4$	$3/4$	$16\,1/2$	
D	2	Ends	Red Oak	$1/4$	$1\,3/4$	$11\,1/2$	
E	2	Ends	Red Oak	$1/4$	$1\,1/2$	11	
F	2	Ends	Red Oak	$1/4$	$1\,1/4$	$10\,1/2$	
#2	2	Ends	Red Oak	$1/4$	$3/4$	11	
G	1	Back	Plywood	$1/4$	12	18	

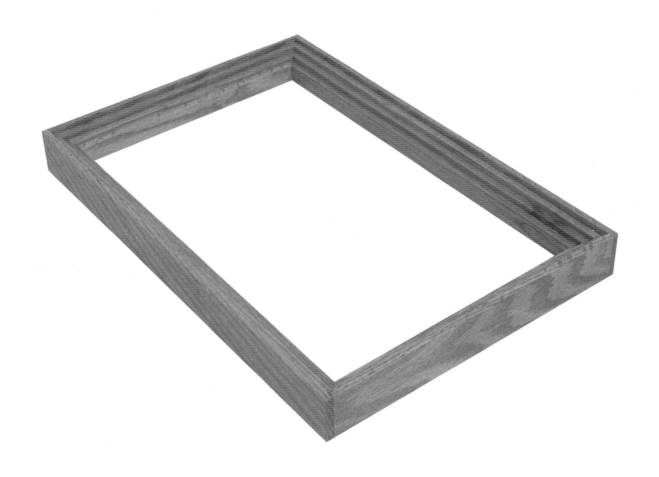

1

Setup for gluing DEF#2 and ABC#1. All of these parts can be glued up at the same time. This makes it easy to fit the corner step-miter joints. (Note the ¼"-thick spacers. These create the space for the mirror or glass.) See cross-section in the illustration.

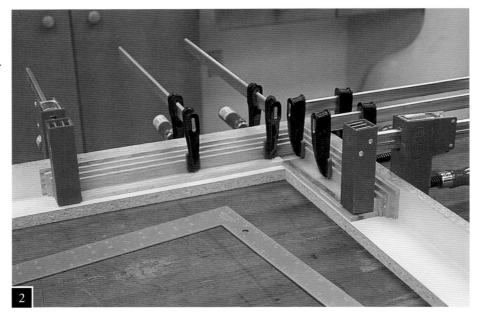

Gluing a top and a side assembly together. Double-check for squareness. Two (2) of these assemblies are needed.

2

Final glue-up of the frame. (Note the spacer used to level the frame with the gluing jig.)

3

index

Fine furniture ideas and more from Popular Woodworking Books!

Authentic Arts & Crafts Furniture Projects
Whatever your skill level, you'll find something special in this beautifully crafted book. Each classic furniture project is taken from the files of Popular Woodworking, the skill-building project magazine for practical woodworkers.
#70499/$24.99/128 pages/200 color images/paperback

Classic Country Furniture
Packed with 20 attractive and functional projects, this guide provides you with the perfect mix of techniques, woods and designs for building country furniture. Fully illustrated steps and instructions accompany each piece, so you can complete projects without any guesswork.
#70475/$19.99/128 pages/250 color images/paperback

How to Build Classic Garden Furniture
This easy, step-by-step guide will have you anxious to begin crafting this elegant outdoor furniture. The 20 projects are designed to withstand years of outdoor exposure with minimal care, and are versatile enough to compliment any home's style. Each beautiful piece is made easy to accomplish with full-color illustrations, numbered steps, close-up photos and alternatives for design, wood selection and finishing. #70395/$24.99/128 pages/275 color, 69 b&w illus./paperback

Quick & Easy Furniture You Can Build with Dimensional Lumber
This book ensures that you get the most for your money when it comes to purchasing and building with framing lumber. It covers every aspect of the furniture-making process with step-by-step instructions, precise measurements, full-color photos, tips and sidebars.
#70459/$22.99/128 pages/250 color images/paperback

25 Essential Projects for Your Workshop
This collection contains some of the most popular projects from Popular Woodworking magazine! Each one has been designed for practical use in the wood shop-clever stands, cabinets, storage devices and more. In addition, helpful "shop tips" are sprinkled throughout each chapter, providing invaluable insight and advice.
#70472/$22.99/128 pages/275 color images/paperback

Tables You Can Customize
Learn how to build four types of basic tables - from a Shaker coffee table to a Stickley library table - then discover how to apply a wide range of variations to customize the pieces to fit your personal needs. #70299/$19.99/128 pages/150 b&w illus./paperback

Desks You Can Customize
Customize your furniture to fit your personal style. With insightful instruction and detailed drawing, you'll create a unique, individualized desk as you experiment with legs, doors, drawers, organizers and much more. #70309/$19.99/128 pages/133 b&w illus./paperback

Display Cabinets You Can Customize
Go beyond building to designing furniture. You'll receive step-by-step instructions to the base projects - the starting points for a wide variety of pieces, such as display cabinets, tables and cases. Then you'll learn about customizing techniques. You'll see how to adapt a glass-front cabinet; put a profile on a cabinet by using molding; get a different look by using stained glass or changing the legs and much more! #70282/$18.99/128 pages/150 b&w illus./paperback

Fast & Easy Techniques for Building Modern Cabinetry
Danny Proulx shows you how to build easy, cost-efficient projects for increasing your storage space. Using basic tools and materials, you'll learn the techniques necessary to build custom cabinets to fit your needs and your home.
#70466/$22.99/128 pages/250 color images/paperback

Building Shelves in a Weekend
In this book, Alan and Gill Bridgewater provide you with 15 step-by-step shelf projects suitable for all levels of experience. Each one clearly shows which wood to use, how much is required, which tools are needed, and how to construct and finish each piece.
#70478/$16.99/80 pages/225+ color images/paperback

Smart Shelving & Storage Solutions
These innovative and inexpensive storage solutions are perfect for do-it-yourselfers. From book shelves, chests and cabinets to armoires, closet systems and benches, you'll find more than 27 woodworking projects to help you make the most of your space - whether it's under the bed, over the sink or in the garage.
#70445/$24.99/144 pages/360 color, 40 b&w illus./paperback

The Weekend Woodworker
A fantastic resource for the straightforward, step-by-step projects you like! This book offers you a range of attractive challenges, from smaller items - such as a stylish CD rack, mailbox or birdhouse - to larger, easy-to-assemble projects including a wall cupboard, child's bed, computer workstation or coffee table. Each project provides clear and easy step-by-step instructions, photographs and diagrams, ideal for both the beginner and expert.
#70456/$22.99/144 pages/200 color photos/paperback

Making More Wooden Mechanical Models
Turn the cranks, press the buttons and pull the levers on 15 projects that make great gifts. Despite their seemingly elaborate configurations, they're simple to make following this guide's complete step-by-step instructions. You'll find that every project features a full-color close up of the finished piece, in addition to hand-rendered drawings, cutting lists and special tips for making difficult steps easier.
#70444/$24.99/128 pages/15 color, 250 b&w illus/paperback

Making Wooden Mechanical Models
Discover plans for 15 handsome and incredibly clever machines with visible wheels, cranks, pistons and other moving parts make of wood. Expertly photographed and complete with materials lists and diagrams, the plans call for a challenging variety of techniques and procedures.
#70288/$21.99/144 pages/341 illus./paperback